GOING TO THE PICTURES: SCOTTISH MEMORIES OF CINEMA

NMS PUBLISHING PRESENTS THE PEOPLE OF SCOTLAND IN

WRITTEN AND DIRECTED BY ANDREW MARTIN

GOING TO THE PICTURES:
SCOTTISH MEMORIES OF CINEMA

WITH BONNIE SCOTLAND: ON THE BIG SCREEN

The Scottish Life Archive at the National Museums of Scotland
holds full texts of the material gathered as part of this project.
Researchers are welcome. It should be remembered that memories
of particular cinemas, films, and dates may be unreliable.

Published by NMS Publishing Limited,
Royal Museum, Chambers Street,
Edinburgh EH1 1JF

British Library Cataloguing in Publication Data
A catalogue record of this book
is available from the British Library.

ISBN 1901663442

Designed by Mark Blackadder.
Printed and bound in the United Kingdom by Bell and Bain Limited, Glasgow

This book would have been impossible without all those who shared their memories – the cast of hundreds.

PHOTOGRAPHS COURTESY OF
SCOTTISH FILM AND
TELEVISION ARCHIVE
AT SCOTTISH SCREEN,
EDINBURGH FILM GUILD,
BRITISH FILM INSTITUTE,
ST ANDREWS PRESERVATION
TRUST MUSEUM,
RCAHMS,
JAMES HOUSTON,
VIOLET CRUICKSHANK,
G B MILLAR,
SCOTTISH LIFE ARCHIVE,
SHETLAND MUSEUM,
PAUL ARCHIBALD,
HELEN GILMOUR,
BILL DOUGLAS CENTRE,
UNIVERSITY OF EXETER,
PAT DENNISON,
SCOTTISH LIFE ARCHIVE,
TOM CHISHOLM,
WILLIAM RAE,
TED TURNER
INTERNATIONAL
AND WALT DISNEY

OTHER PHOTOS TAKEN FROM
THE AUTHOR'S COLLECTION

In addition to those credited in the text, thanks to:

John Adams, Madge Atkinson, Christine Beck, Tom Bee, George Bryson, J Burns, Helen Clayton, Bridget Clint, Ken Cockburn, Trevor Cowie, George Dalgleish, Sarah Dallman, Pat Dennison and Stronsay friends, Pupils of the History Department, Denny High, School, Tom Donald, Edward Donaldson, Winifred Donaldson, Frank Duncan, Marjorie Dunlop, Catherine Emslie, June Galloway, Jean Gilmour, Annette Gilroy, Peter Glancy, Rae Glancy, Ellen Hamilton, Bob Henderson, Valerie Henderson, Irene Henry, Andrew Hopwood, David Hopwood, Alexia Howe, Charles Hunter, John Hunter, Ken Ingles, Lesley Johnson, Laura Johnston, Moira Kilburn, Amy Kinnaird, Pupils of Primary Six, Kippen Primary School, Lamond Laing, Bill Lamb, Colin Liddell, David Litteljohn, Malcolm Lobban, Charlie Lynch, Janet McCran, T W MacFarlane, Archie McGill, J McIllrick, E Mackie, James McKenna, Moira Mackenzie, Patrick McLaughlin, Heather McVean, Eric Malcolm, Catherine Marquis, Angus Martin, George Maughfling, John Melaugh, Margaret Millar, Blair Miller, Jim Mitchell, Margaret Mitchell, Jonathan Muirhead, Jean Murdoch, Lynn Murdoch, Gordon Neil, John Paget, John Paterson, Gavin Philip, William Rae, Valerie Ralston, Jennifer Rattray, Audrey Robb, Gordon Robertson, Wendy Rogers, Stuart Reid, Archie Rennie, Mary Scott, Mary Sinclair, Alister Smith, Jean Smith, W R Smith, M Spinks, Christine Stevenson, Adele Stewart, Marie Stoddart, Erlyn Stout, Emma Taylor, Kenneth Thomson, Agnes Watson, G A Williams, Jean Williams, Jacqueline Williamson, Douglas Wilson, Ruth Wilson.

And to all those on-set who helped to get the show on the road:

Cara Shanley (NMS Publishing), Tom Chisholm, Elaine Edwards, Jim Gallacher, Elizabeth Goring, Dorothy Kidd, Tina Mackay, Emma Robinson, Elize Rowan, Clare Whittaker (NMS), Janet McBain, Anne Docherty (Scottish Film and Television Archive at Scottish Screen), Tommy Watt, Ian Tait (Shetland Museums), Dr Duncan Petrie, Dr

Hester Higton (Bill Douglas Centre for the History of Cinema and Popular Culture, University of Exeter), Cherise Saywell, Helene Telford (Edinburgh Film Guild), Iain Fraser Veronica Steele (RCAHMS), Jamie Hall (NMS Lumière), Julie McSkimming (Edinburgh Festival Theatre), Matthew Jarrow (St Andrews Preservation Trust Museum), Paul Archibald (Lanark Library), Ruth Airley (Dumfries and Galloway Public Libraries), Lorna Mitchell (Perth Library), Janet Klak (Fife Libraries), Judith Bowers (Britannia Music Hall Trust), Alison Fraser (Orkney Library and Archive Service), BBC Radio Scotland, Cinema Theatre Association, and staff of cinemas, museums, libraries and local newspapers throughout Scotland:

Dick Bovington, Frank Bruce, Cynthia Burdell, Michael Cox, Leonard Crooks, Janet Cummings, Alex Dickson, Audrey Farley, Janette Holt, Helen Kemp, James King, Connie Leith, Scott McCutcheon, Fiona McKinlay, Tom Martin, Joe Meloy, Eleanor Pattinson, Bruce Peter, Lee Thorburn, Lynne Ross.

Research on this publication was assisted by a scholarship from the Friends of the National Museums of Scotland.

The significant contribution of the Scottish Film and Television Archive at Scottish Screen to this publication is gratefully acknowledged.

Illustrations: *pages* 120, 122, 133, 134 (British Film Institute); 126, 138, 142, 145 (Edinburgh Film Guild); viii, 29, 76, 118 (Royal Commission for Ancient and Historical Monuments of Scotland); 18, 23, 24, 27, 34, 40, 49, 81, 87, 125, 150, 160 (Scottish Film and Television Archive at Scottish Screen).

CLARK GABLE AND CLAUDETTE COLBERT HITCH A RIDE TO THE OSCARS IN 'IT HAPPENED ONE NIGHT', 1934.

CONTENTS

TROXY

MAGNIFICENT OBSESSION

On a seaside holiday as a child I recall my uncle, pantomiming exhaustion, pausing by a country roadside, pulling up his trouser leg and displaying an inch or so of flesh. I thought for a moment this was something vaguely Masonic. I don't remember now what the passing motorists thought of the engineer's antics, but the rest of the family laughed. They knew instantly that my burly uncle was impersonating the star of a film they had all seen 40 years before. My uncle was being Claudette Colbert, she who displayed her million dollar gams, stopped traffic, and hitched a ride in 'It Happened One Night'. My uncle and auntie, and my mum and dad had spent their youth, like so many Scots, at the pictures.

For those growing up in the 1920s and '30s, and for young adults in the '40s, those were golden days for a social phenomenon which was universal. Like many Scots my mum and dad, aunties and future uncles went to the pictures regularly and indiscriminately. Dad's youthful enthusiasm for Tom Mix would later turn to Gary Cooper adventures and a wartime penchant for Judy Garland and June Allyson. Auntie liked Ronald Colman and Clark Gable – 'sexy' was the word she used in later life. Mum agreed on Colman, but appreciated the gentle romanticism of Leslie Howard, and later Paul Henreid, as well as the well-tailored form of Cary Grant. 'They don't make men like that now,' she would say. There were great ladies to admire and emulate too: the elegance of Norma Shearer; Joan Fontaine's simple jumper and pearls; Bette Davis in a hat with a veil. As the War years came, the youngest auntie, a brunette, would abandon the Film Star Club ceremonies in the back garden, model herself on Hedy Lamarr, but paint her toenails à la Betty Grable.

THE TROXY, LEVEN, Family tales and myths brought the world of Hollywood right down to
DESIGNED BY A D HAXTON. the familiarity of Dumfries – the Electric, the Regal and the Lyceum. Bebe
(RCAHMS)

Daniels, said to be from Texas, was the same Daniels as the chemist in Buccleuch Street. Will Rogers was a school-fellow of Grandfather's. Douglas Fairbanks was shooting on an estate close by. A girl in Thornhill post office had stared into his blue eyes. And a local mansion's leafy grounds sheltered – could it be? – Jessie Matthews and other wartime stars too fragile for the harsh times.

The War changed things. Young people left home and saw sights they would never forget, far afield from Dumfries. Dad watched films under the Algerian stars, and in Italy missed Clark Gable, who was close by. Mum, with the Civil Service in London, spent precious shillings on tinned salmon sandwiches and a trip away from her hostel to the Empire, Leicester Square, for 'Gone With The Wind'.

And then marriage, and family, and picture-going became an occasional treat; no longer a central part of life. 'That must've been before 1953,' my mother would say, remembering an old film on television. 'I never went to the pictures after we were married' – as if Dad had a hand in preventing her.

This book is made up of memories from hundreds of Scots, ample proof of the part cinema played in ordinary people's lives for at least the first six decades of the twentieth century. For many it was the stars who mattered most – distant glamorous objects of affection or admiration, laughing, fighting, or loving in make-believe worlds – all set in an art deco palace of pleasure where the price of the ticket bought you a night out with a good pal or a prospective mate. For people like Mum and Dad, the Regals and the Odeons took them to a world that had little to do with the realities of life. It was an entertainment, an education, an experience, and an escape.

Like all good entertainments this book is a double feature. The supporting programme concerns Scots and Scotland on the screen. You will have to provide your own refreshments, and the National Anthem will not be played at the end. So join the queue. Seats in all parts.

Andrew Martin

LEFT TO RIGHT: BEBE DANIELS (CIGARETTE CARD, 1928), DOLORES DEL RIO (CIGARETTE CARD, 1934), LORETTA YOUNG (CINEMA FOYER PORTRAIT, CIRCA 1938).

BABES IN ARMS:
THE EARLY DAYS OF CINEMA IN SCOTLAND

Cinema came to Scotland at a time when the invention was spanking new and sweeping the world. London had Britain's very first screening in February 1896, and Edinburgh's Empire Theatre followed on 13 April, but few then were very impressed by the phenomenon, advertised as the greatest novelty of the age. *The Scotsman* said, 'unfortunately last night the exhibition somehow missed fire'. By all accounts the audience at the Empire was better pleased by the variety acts on the bill than the flickering images of dancing, boxing, a shoe-black, a policeman and a sailor – though *The Scotsman* critic conceded that the cockfight was exceedingly good. The management may have apologised for the quality that night, but these first moving images from Edison's Kinetoscope had extraordinary significance. There had been peepshows before, but the first moving pictures added an important dimension – this was a public, not private, entertainment to a paying audience, and the pictures were projected onto a screen.

Cinema's Scottish debut may not have been a smash, but within weeks and months a variety of different versions of the Kinetoscope were to be seen all over the country. The Lumière Cinematographe appeared at the Empire in June and played for a week to great acclaim, with its programme including 'Dinner Hour At The Factory' and 'Arrival Of The Paris Express'. In Glasgow the Britannia Music Hall débuted with the Lumière Brothers too, and a rival British system, invented by Robert Paul, did well in Aberdeen. Glasgow's Theatre Royal showed 'A Trip To The Moon' as the interval attraction of its 'Robinson Crusoe' pantomime, and audiences were transfixed by the colour and trick effects.

EMPIRE PALACE THEATRE, EDINBURGH, AS IT WAS AT THE TIME OF THE FIRST SCREENING, 1896. (EDINBURGH FESTIVAL THEATRE)

Entrepreneurs hastily added film to their variety shows in the cities and on tour, so that town and village halls and fairs all over the country got a chance to show the flickering images to rural Scots. These films were short – a few minutes long – with subjects which today might seem very ordinary indeed, but the wonder was that moving pictures lit up the darkness and looked like life. Queen Victoria saw films at Balmoral and appeared on screen herself in the Diamond Jubilee festivities, and featured in 1901 at her State Funeral.

The new phenomenon was popular and cheap, and the penny gaff was largely looked upon as an amusement for the lower classes. Early cinemas reflected this, as most were hasty conversions from other premises with basic seating, in heavily populated areas of Scottish cities. Old shops, halls, factories and Turkish baths had benches installed – many were genuine fleapits; some were fire hazards. The day of the plush Picture Palace was many years away. Drunks and prostitutes were often regulars, but so were families – it kept the children out of over-crowded homes, off the streets and in the warmth, and for husbands it was cheaper than a night in the pub. By 1915 Edinburgh had nearly 40 cinemas.

In 1910 the Kinematograph Act attempted to make the halls safer – fire had been a constant hazard. Now there would be regulations on construction materials and fire-proofing. New cinemas would be more comfortable and more attractive to a respectable audience. The authorities were shocked to find that women and children attended Electric Theatres unaccompanied. Cinemas, for the first time purpose-built, became a familiar sight in the High Street, often as an elaborate shop-front or as a handsome piece of architecture – as in Campbeltown's Picture House, opened in 1913.

A seal of approval was bestowed on the medium, it was said, by the appearance of Sarah Bernhardt, the world's greatest actress as 'Camille' in

1908. It was, she said, her chance for immortality. By 1913, when Edinburgh's Palladium featured her as 'Queen Bess' for a top price of sixpence, cinema was practically an art form. European films were widely seen. France had its comics, and Italy had epics such as 'Cabiria' and 'Quo Vadis?'. The whole world – including the King and Queen at the Albert Hall, and the people of Wishaw – could enjoy the spectacle of Christians being thrown to the lions, and pagans caught in a volcanic eruption.

The first feature film, 'The Great Train Robbery' – all of ten minutes long – had been made near New York in 1903, and within a few years an industry had sprung up in America which was to dominate the world. The star system was born, and its first success was Florence Lawrence, named as 'The Biograph Girl' in 1910 (now remembered, not for any film, but for that tag alone). When she left for a rival studio, her title was inherited by the erstwhile 'Girl with the Curls' who eclipsed her – Mary Pickford. Little Mary was a universal screen phenomenon. What Mary did twice-nightly could attract the locals in Haddington; fishermen in Kintyre went ashore tae find whit happened tae her, and Pickford could demand a million-dollar contract. The First World War confirmed Hollywood, a small California town with orange trees in the streets and coyotes in the hills, as the focus of the film industry.

Here are the memories of Scots who remember the Silents, starting with a legendary tale of early cinema, retold by someone who had it first-hand from a manager father.

Mary Pickford

Dorothy Vernon of Haddon Hall

Two elderly ladies were making their very first visit to a cinema and took their seats not far from the screen in the centre of the stalls. One scene caused them to panic. The film was of a train coming towards the audience, gathering speed on the railway track … this made the two ladies start screaming and they left their seats and raced up the side passage with the usherette running after them, telling them it was only a film, and that there was no train in the cinema.

BILLIE WILSON

My dad first went to the pictures about 1914. He had no idea what was in store, but remembered seeing cowboys flickering about on a dirty white sheet. He was not the least impressed by this moving-picture business the posters kept advertising.

WALTER WATT

In those days in Aberdeen it was the Silents, with letters printed on the screen telling us what the stars were saying. The quietness in the cinema could be a tonic in itself – with a pianist, or perhaps an orchestra playing and often a man reading the words. On a cold night in the warmth of the cinema you might fall asleep, or if you were lonely it was always somewhere to go.

VIOLET CRUICKSHANK

In 1924 as a birthday surprise, my father took me to the New Kinema in Aberdeen. I do not remember the name of the film, but I was entranced nevertheless. From that time on, I became a regular visitor. I remember attending many a Saturday afternoon matinée at the Electric, the main feature (or as it was known, the 'big picture') being a Western starring one of many cowboys – Tom Mix, Buck Jones, Hoot Gibson, Ken Maynard, Fred Thompson or Tim McCoy. Other films I recall viewing were 'Beau Geste' with handsome Ronald Colman, 'Seventh Heaven' with adorable Janet Gaynor, and 'Wings' with 'It Girl' Clara Bow. Even as a child, one was discerning as to favourite stars. Being a boy, my favourites consisted mainly of males such as Richard Barthelmess, Richard Dix and Colman.

JOHN ALLAN

A religious epic was usually considered respectable viewing for all the family. It also provided spectacle, excitement, and the chance to look at handsome men unclothed.

I'm sure my grandma and I saw 'Ben-Hur' on each of five evenings. The manager had devised sound effects – for example a hand-revolved barrel with chains inside for the chariot race. My grandmother was the subject of some teasing about falling in love with Ramon Novarro, the screen idol of the time, in the title role.

HELEN GILMOUR

All hands were called upon to add sound and atmosphere …

'The Sea Hawk' was a grand pirate picture. It had the accompaniment of the orchestra playing many musical pieces as the story unfolded on screen. I took part with Dad and some of the staff on stage at side of the screen, unseen by the audience of course. For the thunder, the doorman shook a large piece of metal, the heavy rain was a large wooden box of dried peas, and it really sounded like there was a heavy

rainfall. For horses racing along, Steve the usher (with only one arm) and myself had horseshoes gripped in our hands. From our kneeling positions we galloped on the wooden floor. I guess no one realised it was a three-legged horse.

BILLIE WILSON

As a family we moved to Paisley from the country in 1920. Aged eleven, I was the eldest of three and, like my sisters (aged eight and five), preferred the country life. However the cinema was an exciting bonus, and on Saturday mornings I was given our picture money to cover the cost of the matinée and sweeties – sixpence. A penny each for the cinema, and three pence for broken chocolate.

One Saturday the serial was so intense, and everyone so still and quiet, that I got a fright when Kitty the elder sister nudged me. Irritated, I shooshed her. But she persisted and whispered 'Chrissie's crying, she couldn't help doing the toilet'. I thought that so funny – then worried about those below. But the balcony was well-made.

ALBERT BURNAP

Brought up in the cinema by a manager father, a daughter of the trade remembers the silent days …

Orchestras played a large part in the atmosphere of a film. The pianist, cellist, violinist and drummer – the orchestra – sat immediately in front of the screen and as the film was running they played appropriate music for the scene being shown. Rousing music for battles, horses galloping and sword-fighting. Waltzes and sweet music for love scenes and weepy parts. There were rehearsals – always on the Monday morning of the change of film, and the orchestra watched carefully with the leader, the pianist, and pieces of music were discussed, so as to choose the best ones to use.

BILLIE WILSON

My Uncle Bill managed the Playhouse in Aberdeen back in the days of the silent pictures. Part of his job involved speaking over the Silents and doing dramatic readings and the like before the main picture. His wife was called Gladys and she worked as an elocutionist, but also alongside him doing speaking at the Playhouse as a sideline.

We always tried to avoid them like the plague, since she was the type who would say in a loud voice 'Hello Dahlings', to our huge embarrassment. I have no idea how she went down with your average Aberdeen audience.

DOROTHY DAVIDSON

Outside the cities, cinemas were never really silent either, not when local talents could be called upon.

Silent films in Oban were set to live music to fit the action on the screen, such as galloping horses in a Cowboys and Indians film, or a sentimental love scene which we all whistled at, down in the threepenny seats. The music was provided by Mr Strain, the church organist, on the piano and Miss Lemon on the violin. Mr Strain always wore a cloak which hung from his shoulders.

NEAL QUINN

For children, visiting the cinema could have its hazards as well as pleasures. Harold Lloyd, for instance, was always finding himself hanging from tall buildings …

If the films were silent, the audiences certainly were not. My cousin tended to get carried away with the escapades of Harold Lloyd and on one occasion, climbing with Harold up the face of a building, my cousin rose gradually from his seat. Consequently when Harold slipped, Bert had to pick himself up from the floor.

CHARLIE CHAPLIN
PANTOMIMES, 1927.

HELEN GILMOUR

Cinemas were often rudimentary, as these memories from Dundee in the 1920s relate.

I lived in Lyon Street and just had to turn the corner and cross the road to the Royal where all my first memories took place. It had an earth floor with forms at the front but seats at the back. When I was with my father we sat in the seats; when I was with my chums we sat at the front as near as possible to the piano lady. These piano ladies I hero-worshipped. They watched the screen all the time, yet whether the film was sad or funny they could change the tune instantly.

If there was a film of Harold Lloyd or Charlie Chaplin showing, men with big papier mâché heads would hand out publicity leaflets outside school. In those days my favourites, apart from them, were Wallace Beery, Jackie Coogan, Tom Mix and

Douglas Fairbanks. Pearl White always left you dying to get back on Saturday afternoon to see if she was rescued before the train ran over her or the rope broke and she fell hundreds of feet to the bottom.

MAY COOK

For ordinary people the cinema could provide a quiet night out in comfort.

My mother had been following 'Maria Marten' in a magazine and wanted to see it. We were a poor family, my father and brother both unemployed, and I only remember her ever being at the pictures twice. If you cut the coupons from the 'Lyons Tea' packet you got into the cinema free, so off we went, but my mother did not want anyone to see us getting in, so we had to hang about a bit outside. At last we got in and found good seats. My mother, not being used to sitting comfy and doing nothing (and enjoying the tinkling piano), fell asleep during the first picture and saw nothing of 'Maria Marten'. When I turned round at the end to say how good it was, she awoke. Well, I got punched in the back all the way home, really hard. I was threatened with far worse if I told them at home what had happened.

MAY COOK

But it was not everybody's idea of a good night out …

One Saturday I managed to encourage my grandmother to go to the pictures. She thought it such a waste of time, just sitting there watching people on a screen, when she could have been knitting her sock. In those days old ladies could knit a sock in the dark, they didn't need to see the stitches.

ISABELLE SHAW

Two of the great leading ladies of the early screen feature in this memory from Kirkcaldy. Gish is well-remembered today, mostly for her work with D W Griffith; but Talmadge, a prestigious romantic star from before World War I until the coming of the Talkies, is often forgotten.

I remember when I was 16, a boy asked me for a date. The hall in Commercial Street was showing pictures at that time. The picture was 'Smilin Through' and the star was Norma Talmadge. The pianist played throughout. Another picture from my teens was at the Rialto. It was 'The White Sister', with Lillian Gish. You had to take a handkerchief with you to see her pictures, they were always so sad. She was a nun. There was an earthquake and some bits were frightening, but we sat through it.

CATHERINE JARVIS

My first visit to the cinema, about 1921, was to see 'Nanook Of The North' in a Princes Street picture house, possibly the New. I was far too young to understand much and was mainly terrified by what I saw on the screen. All I can remember is the blizzard and the building of the igloo – when that word appeared on the screen, although I could not read, I found the shapes of the letters menacing. But what impressed me most was the atmosphere – the darkness and the rich smells of chocolate and cigars.

MAY WILLIAMSON

In about 1925, my uncle took me to my first evening performance at the local cinema. I was about nine years old. The film was 'The Kid', with Charlie Chaplin and Jackie Coogan. I was intrigued by my introduction to local night-life but most of all by the sheer magic of Chaplin. What I remember was that on the film there was permanent rain that showered down inside and out. No one seemed surprised or deterred by it. It was many years before I realised the film must have been worn out. Years later I was enthralled by 'The Gold Rush' and 'City Lights', but nothing ever approached the thrill of seeing a film where the rain never stopped!

THOMAS LING

My father worked as a bookbinder in Aberdeen, but during the evenings he played the violin at the Torry Cinema. It could easily have got away with having only a pianist, but instead it had a reasonably sized orchestra. Eventually he led the orchestra and would always play a solo piece during the interval. My mother worked at the bookbinders too, and she'd taken a shine to my father. So, every night – except Sunday of course – she would go to the Torry cinema just to admire him from a distance.

They married and my father moved to the much bigger La Scala in the centre of Aberdeen, with an even bigger orchestra. That only lasted a few years though, because the Talkies were coming in and as soon as they arrived at La Scala, my father had to find a new job. All the city cinemas went over to sound, so he had to move. He ended up in Macduff where there was only one cinema – still silent. So he spent a year there leading the orchestra – then it too got sound equipment, and he was out of work. He returned to Aberdeen, back to bookbinding.

BILL COOPER

JACKIE COOGAN

15

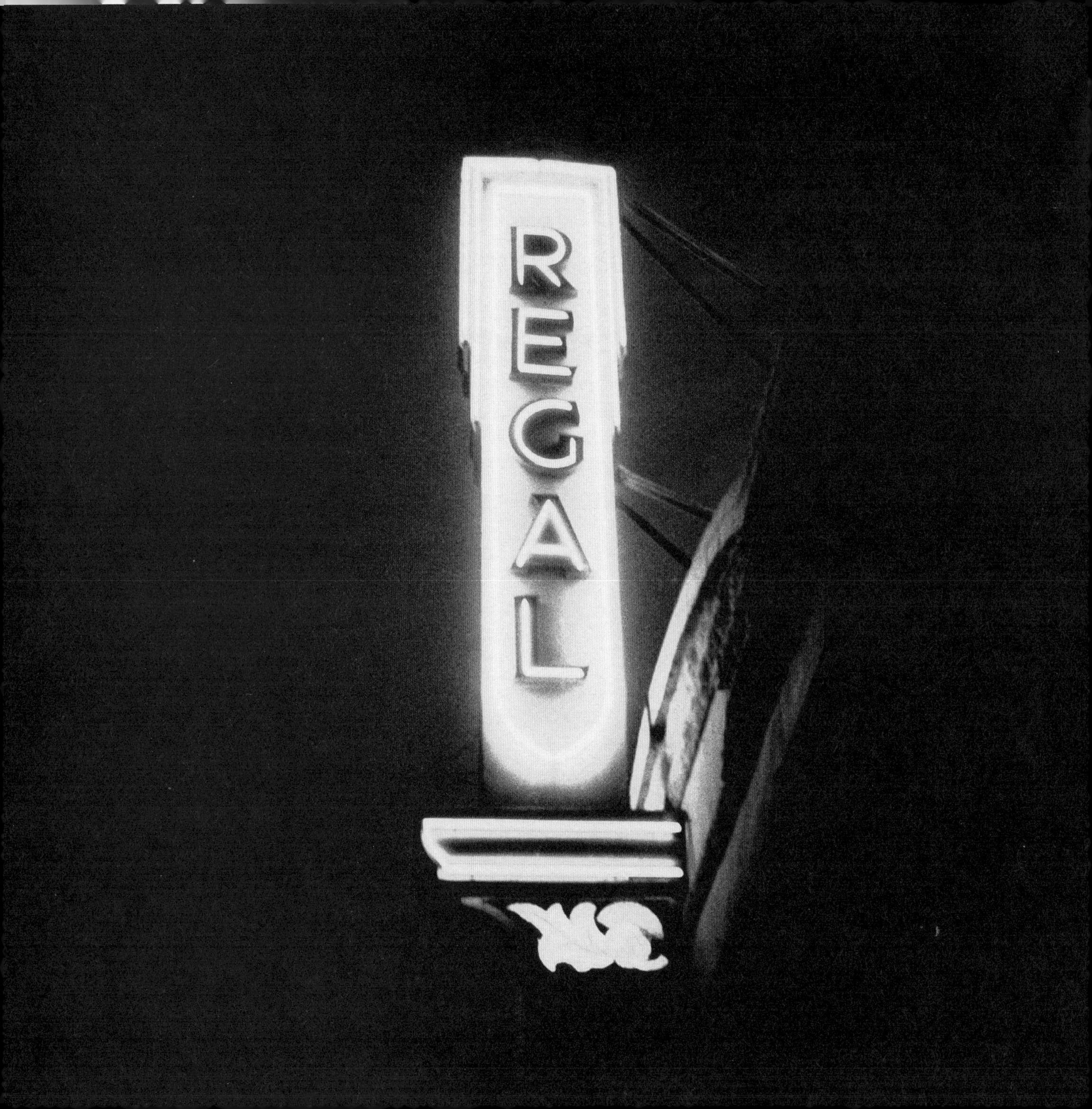
REGAL

SAY IT WITH SONGS:
TALKIES COME TO SCOTLAND

Wonder of wonders, then came the Talkies!

MARGARET CHRISTIE

Experimental sound films had been around for many years, but had never quite caught on, when in 1926 Warner Brothers persevered, for purely financial reasons, to avert a studio crisis. They gambled on synchronised effects and music, presenting John Barrymore as 'Don Juan'. There was no dialogue, but plenty of clashing swords. It screened with supporting musical shorts, and the feature's success encouraged the studio to play about on a grander scale with their innovatory sound system Vitaphone.

The coming of the Talkies to Scotland is a significant memory for older cinema-goers. Everybody remembers Al Jolson, a Broadway performer who thus secured himself a place in cinema history. His Talkie debut was 'The Jazz Singer' in 1927, basically a silent film with his hit songs and a few famous words. It changed the industry. For many audiences however, Jolson's real Talkie sensation was 'The Singing Fool', which arrived in Scotland in January 1929. At Glasgow's Coliseum, business was so hectic that legend says there was a queue extending all the way to Charing Cross, and tram passengers alighted accordingly. As cinemas all over the country converted to sound, this was the feature that many managers craved, and Scots flocked to see Jolson belt out his repertoire in black-face. He sang 'Sonny Boy' to Davey Lee, and audiences wept. Managers wept on their way to the Bank of Scotland.

THE REGAL, MACDUFF BY NIGHT.
(G B MILLAR)

Jolson's impact in this and similar roles was repeated throughout the land. Here is what happened in Grantown-on-Spey:

17

My parents were astounded to find crowds streaming into the picture house to see Al Jolson. My father ran all the way back to our house, and I was wakened by him saying 'Hurry up and get dressed, you are going to see the first ever Talkie picture'. We made our way to the back row of the 3d and 6d seats. I can remember Jolson was a man in a tuxedo with a blackened face, painted white lips and white gloves. I cannot recall the story. At the end of the performance – silence. It was all so emotional.

LUCINDA ALLAN

I was about nine or ten at the time, and during the showing my mother sniffled and cried – much of the time to my intense embarrassment. A movie that was a tear-jerker, and Jolson singing 'Sonny Boy', was not to be taken lightly. Not a Kleenex in the house – mostly linen or cotton handkerchiefs.

JOHN ALLAN

Even Talkies could outstay their welcome however.

I had an uncle from Kyle of Lochalsh who used to come to Inverness every Saturday to see my future aunt. As he couldn't see her until she had finished work, it was me he took to 'the movies', as he called them. The Playhouse had just opened, and one of the first pictures was 'The Singing Fool' with Al Jolson and a little boy. The big song was 'Sonny Boy' and soon afterwards my mother threatened to shoot me if I sang it one more time.

MEGAN CATHCART

Sound caused mayhem in the studios on both sides of the Atlantic. Quality nose-dived as completed Silents were given music tracks, or a few moments of talk, or were re-shot from scratch. Some films, like 'The Singing Fool', were released as half-and-half. Cameras could no longer rove at will, static camera work became the rule, and merciless microphones were stuck under the noses of actors who had never read a line in their lives.

Song and chatter abounded in the first years of Talkies, unimaginatively shot and imperfectly recorded. But did the audiences stay away? Off screen the cash registers jingled, queues formed, and cinemas without funds to convert to sound began to close. Orchestras looked for other work, and the years of the piano player were over – Talkies were here to stay.

Scottish cinema managers rushed to install the new system. The first Talkies employed synchronised sound courtesy of gramophone discs – one side to one reel. In theory, lips moved in time with the words on the disc, but often this went astray: needles stuck in grooves, projectionists became flustered, and, in her Talkie debut, Norma Shearer could be seen and heard speaking her leading man's dialogue.

Billie Wilson was a very interested little girl, watching the changeover in the King's Playhouse, Montrose:

This was really a wonderful happening in our lives. Fred was the RCA boss who came to supervise the installation. He was very 'American' but nice, and it must have been difficult for him, especially as he could only work before and after the show, when there were no audiences in the hall. He was often working during the night and weekends, as everything had to be absolutely correct. At the same time he was coaching the chief operator in the intricacies of this new wonder – the talking pictures. One Saturday, it was all together and ready to try out.

At each side of the large stage were mounted speakers which stood high up, almost to top of auditorium. Now everything was ready for showing to all who were

invited – news reporters and various folk of the town who wanted to be first to see this wonderful Talkie. Dad's cinema was the first local hall to have such a thing. A run-through of the sound was made and we were all staring at the turntable as it turned the large discs. These were just like you had with your gramophone, except instead of the arm with the needle starting at the outside of disc, you started at the inside and the disc turned until it reached the outside. This was to be one of the more difficult things. The timing of the film and the sound record had to match exactly or (as everyone found out) you would perhaps have the male lead talking as the female, and of course the female lead speaking as the male. The first machine record would have sides one and three, giving time to rewind the film on the machine and turn to the appropriate sound. The second machine would have sides two and four, and when one forgot to turn the record on none of the sound co-ordinated with the acting at all.

Firstly, there was a short film of musicians (one a pianist and one a violinist) playing, and singing and comedy. The violinist recited 'Mary Had A Little Lamb' by sliding his fingers up and down the violin strings and using his bow across the strings. It really was very clearly a recitation of the nursery rhyme. He timed his bowing to the rhythm of the words. Needless to say, everyone applauded generously at seeing the film and hearing the sound. The first film Dad had was not 'The Singing Fool', as it had been held over again and again in Glasgow. It was 'The Barker', a film of showground people. So the changeover from silent films to Talkies became a reality.

BILLIE WILSON

The early musicals also made use of Technicolor, in a process based on a limited palette. At its best it could be stylish, which suited the unrealistic world of the musical – but there were no shades of blue.

I remember going to see my first colour film, only it was all orange and green. It was 'Sally', with Marilyn Miller and Joe E Brown, around 1931. He was a cook in a café making pancakes, but letting the batter run over as he watched the girls pass by.

MABEL CUNNINGHAM

The first big operetta was the screen version of Sigmund Romberg's tuneful piece of desert fancy. John Boles was the Red Shadow, and playing the exotic Azuri was Myrna Loy. The combination of melody and Technicolor has kept its memory alive, at least in Aberdeen.

My first visit to any cinema was around 1929, when I saw 'The Desert Song' with my parents. From then on I was hooked.

WILLIAM COOPER

At the Queen's we sat around and saw 'The Desert Song' three times. There were four of us and we moved our seats in between each show so that the usherettes wouldn't turf us out. I also well remember the panic our parents were in. They forbade the pictures for a couple of Saturdays.

DOROTHY GARSIDE

In the early days everybody had a go at a song, and an early Fox musical where Janet Gaynor (a very big star with a very small voice) gamely tackled the score, is still a vivid memory.

THE REGAL, BALLATER. (SCOTTISH FILM AND TELEVISION ARCHIVE AT SCOTTISH SCREEN)

I was taken to the pictures for the first time to see Janet Gaynor in 'Sunny Side Up' at the Astoria. Ma must have been on tenderhooks that I would resort to howling the place down. The theme song of the film, 'Keep Your Sunny Side Up, Up …' was often sung by Ma, and today, almost 70 years later, I can still whistle the tune, but can remember only the first line.

GEORGE BAIRD

The other great hit from that picture was tellingly 'If I Had A Talking Picture Of You'. Audiences throughout the world sang along. Hollywood ransacked Broadway for directors, writers and actors familiar with talk. Some of the most famous names of later years took the train west and faced up to the camera. In Scotland, where there had always been a suspicion that the cinema was not quite respectable, there was an extra concern – American culture.

For the first time Transatlantic accents were widely heard, and ridiculed. Audiences spoke back to the actors. Would those nasal tones rub off on the populace of Scotland?

THE GREATEST SHOW ON EARTH:
A NIGHT AT THE PICTURES

*I can close my eyes and see these Palaces of Romance once again. The foyer
started the tingle once we had bought our tickets – fitted carpets (such luxury),
and large studio portraits of the current screen idols. I often wondered what
happened to all those wonderful pictures. Everyone was perfection
(unlike Cromwell and most of us), with no warts at all.*

ZENA EUNSON

*The silver screen and golden dreams helped us all to weather the hard times. It was
either that or sitting under the gas mantle in those far-off 1930s. Clyde Street
mothers straight across from the La La didn't bother to change and settled down in
their favourite seats, still with their slippers on.*

MATT BYRNE

GREEN'S PLAYHOUSE, DUNDEE.
(SCOTTISH FILM AND
TELEVISION ARCHIVE
AT SCOTTISH SCREEN)

Scotland took to the pictures in a big way. By 1929, just as Talkies were
arriving in the cities, Aberdeen had 15 cinemas, Airdrie had four, Dundee
had 24, Edinburgh 33, Falkirk had seven, and Glasgow 113. There were
three cinemas in Hawick, two in Stranraer and one in Lerwick. Most small
towns had at least one Picture House or Electric; even Lochgelly had its
Cinema De Luxe.

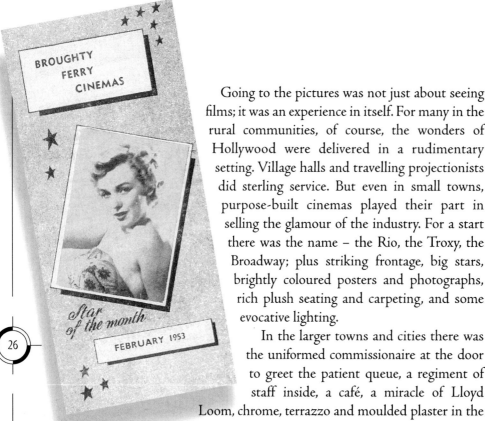

Star of the month

FEBRUARY 1953

Going to the pictures was not just about seeing films; it was an experience in itself. For many in the rural communities, of course, the wonders of Hollywood were delivered in a rudimentary setting. Village halls and travelling projectionists did sterling service. But even in small towns, purpose-built cinemas played their part in selling the glamour of the industry. For a start there was the name – the Rio, the Troxy, the Broadway; plus striking frontage, big stars, brightly coloured posters and photographs, rich plush seating and carpeting, and some evocative lighting.

In the larger towns and cities there was the uniformed commissionaire at the door to greet the patient queue, a regiment of staff inside, a café, a miracle of Lloyd Loom, chrome, terrazzo and moulded plaster in the foyer and auditorium, ice-cream to buy and live music to listen to. And all the way through, on the walls and up the stairs, would be the faces of the remote gods and goddesses central to the popular cinema-going experience.

In the heyday of cinema, studios had an instantly recognised product. MGM provided the most prestigious of dramas. It had Garbo and Gable, Tracy and Crawford. Later it danced and sang without rival. Paramount was the glamorous home of sophisticated comedy: Cooper, Colbert and Crosby. RKO had Astaire and Rogers. Warners had tough guys, swashbucklers, and emotion – Cagney, Flynn, and Davis. Fox had dark-haired men and blonde women – Power and Grable, and a penchant for the gay nineties. Universal had something else – cut-price sets and Boris Karloff.

There was a lot more to enjoy than simply films.

MARILYN MONROE IN THE FIRST YEAR OF HER STARDOM, ALREADY POPULAR ON TAYSIDE. (WILLIAM RAE)

It was normal practice in those days in Edinburgh in the 1940s, especially on a Saturday, to have to queue to get in. It was not unknown to stand outside the Rutland or the Synod Hall for 30 minutes or even an hour. A bit boring, but usually we would be amused by various street entertainers who would make a living going round the cinema queues. They were of varying talents – mostly singers – but the one that sticks in my mind was a youngish fellow who tore paper for a living! His pièce de résistance was to take a newspaper, tear it to bits, then pull it from between his fingers to form a paper ladder which he kept pulling until it reached a height of eight or nine feet. Brilliant!

JOHN WILLIAMSON

There was the bonneted and shawled old lady with the hand-wound gramophone in Leith Walk. I always thought she was a poor old soul until I was told she had made a pile during the War handing out the addresses of good-time girls in the vicinity to visiting GIs. And the several apparently blind musicians who walked along so pitifully playing their sorrowful saxophone or squeezing their melancholy melodeon – see them later sprinting to catch a tram to the dogs at Powderhall or to beat closing time.

JIM BRUNTON

THE CAFE AT THE
CAPITOL, ABERDEEN.
(SCOTTISH FILM AND
TELEVISION ARCHIVE
AT SCOTTISH SCREEN)

A further innovation in the 1930s was the advent of the illuminated cinema organ. I recall attending Aberdeen's Capitol on the day it opened, which I believe was a

Saturday in 1936, and the movie being shown was 'Letty Lynton', starring Joan Crawford and Robert Montgomery. The interior of this new fully carpeted and comfortable theatre was quite breathtaking – especially when, arising from the depths at the front of the cinema, came into view this beautifully illuminated Compton organ. It was a fascinating sight, well worth the one shilling backstalls admission. Smoking was permitted, and immediately attached to the seat facing one was an oval ashtray. As a result, a haze of smoke appeared in the lights thrown by the projector. As a follow-up to the smoke and other inhalants, a cinema attendant would go around the passages with a spray which emitted a perfumed scent.

JOHN ALLAN

THE BATTLE OF LARGS COMMEMORATED IN JAMES HOUSTON'S DESIGN. (RCAHMS)

In Forfar, entertainment was less glamorous, but fun …

A feature of the Pavilion was the community singing before the show, led by Jimmy Scott in evening dress, presiding with his torch dancing the light along the lines shown on the screen. Later my little brother and I used to lie in bed in the dark and dance our torches along imaginary lines while we sang songs. My mother wondered why the batteries went so quickly.

JEAN DUNDAS

In one of Edinburgh's classier halls, now the Odeon, the niceties were still observed …

One evening an otherwise prim-looking old lady sitting next to me in the New Victoria stalls hawked slowly and thoroughly, to my mounting nausea. She then spat deliberately into an envelope which she sealed and carefully placed in her handbag – neither the film nor my companion held further charm for me from that moment, as I sat and wondered if the envelope was stamped and addressed.

JIM BRUNTON

Audiences could get very stuck in their habits …

On a Sunday night in Largs' Viking everybody, literally, had their own seats each and every week. This didn't matter in the winter but one summer night, sitting up in the back of the balcony as the lights went down, I noticed on the opposite side and at the back of the next row, a couple of tourists had sat down. On a bright summer Sunday night, one didn't expect tourists – and though we were the only people in the balcony, they had to sit in these two seats. Sure enough, the credits rolling, a lady of middle years – a housekeeper perhaps, who always had her Sunday night off at the pictures? – arrived, and made the tourists move out of her seat!

DONALD KELLY

Rin Tin Tin was as popular as the glamour queens of the screen, which perhaps accounts for this night out in Galloway …

My grandfather and his friend went together to the pictures in Kirkcudbright every Saturday night with their dogs. That would be the 1930s. One Saturday night they did not go and my grandfather's dog went alone – he was found up in the balcony in their usual seats.

MEG WALKER

Some were unfamiliar with the rituals …

My grandfather (who had a poultry farm near Dollar) came to Kirkcaldy for a visit, and as a treat was taken to the Rio. He was a tall man – over six feet – and had a good sense of humour. I don't remember the film, but when it was over, he turned to me and said, 'Lassie, these seats are awfu' hard'. I looked over and discovered he had never put the seat down.

MARGARET MELDRUM

THERE'S ALWAYS TIME FOR A 'STAR'

-before the 'Show' starts

WILLS'S
STAR
CIGARETTES
10 for 4° 15 for 6° 30 (in box) 1/-
PLAIN OR CORK TIPPED

And other novices brought disaster in their wake ...

Our picture house in Peterhead was the lovely old Music Hall which had a sad ending. My father was a sea-going engineer who never went to the pictures and we always said that if he ever did go, the place would burn down. Anyway, Gracie Fields was showing, so off my father went on a Saturday night. Early next morning the Empress dance hall next door caught fire, spread to the Music Hall, and it was destroyed. Don't think my father ever went to the pictures again!

MARGARET CHRISTIE

I don't think my generation ever appreciated what we got for our money! We regularly got two big pictures, a short comedy (often with Zasu Pitts), a cartoon, a newsreel, forthcoming attractions, local adverts and very often a stage-show half-way through – usually a yodeller or unlikely contortionists, more mind-boggling than a troupe of acrobats. Or the Hammond organ would appear from the depths and accompany us while we sang the words up on the screen, complete with bouncing ball. The programmes usually started about 2 pm and were continuous till probably 10.30 pm. I never did get round to sitting the whole way through – hunger drove me home! That is, not until 'Gone With The Wind' was showing at the Playhouse in the city. The office crowd all climbed up to The Gods and watched this marvellous film on what seemed like a postage stamp screen, we were so high up. At the half-way mark everybody got out their flasks and sandwiches.

STANFORD McNAUGHT

These were the great days of the movies. We soaked it all up and repeated the dialogue next day in the school shelters; tapped and sang the musicals. As we left the cinema in summer, the sun would nip our eyes and we would pile into Rossi's for an ice-cream cone before we climbed Anne Street and home. In winter we would walk up Garscube Road to the mussel shop and buy a penny-worth of the bree, and if we were really flush, a tub of hot peas.

MARION CARRINGTON

AUGUST, 1942

Ritz Cinema
Ayr

NEW RD. 'Phone 2997
Resident Manager—JOHN GILMOUR

NEW PRICES:
Front Stalls, 10d; Back Stalls, 1/3; Balcony, 1/6.
Children accompanied by Parents, 6d, 9d, & 1/-.
No Children's Prices after 4 p.m. on Saturdays
and Holidays.
Free Car Park at rear of Cinema—
enter from Peebles Street.

My first diary entry for January 1st 1947 does not tell of a typical Scottish New Year's Day – we went to the pictures twice. My mother, sister and I left Shawlands on the south side of Glasgow for the Paramount in Renfield Street, to see 'Great Expectations' with John Mills. What an apt title. We might well have won the War but it wasn't immediately obvious. Because our homes were so cold, our regular habit was to go the cinema two or three times a week to keep warm. Tightly packed in the halls, surrounded by a thick cloud of cigarette smoke, was where we wanted to be to relax and forget.

VALERIE SMITH

FROM THE LOCAL PRESS.
(HELEN GIMLOUR)

32

Audiences cheerfully saw everything on offer, the pinnacles as well as the nadir of screen art.

After seeing the film 'Citizen Kane' in March 1942, I noted in my diary that I thought it was rotten; a few days later I saw Abbot and Costello in 'Ride Em Cowboy' and voted it 'sticking out' – that is very good.

GEORGE BAIRD

A bag of chipped fruit helped to make an appropriate conclusion to an evening with the Latin American bombshell famous for her tutti-frutti headgear.

I have a very happy memory of a Carmen Miranda picture at the Blue Halls, Lauriston – on the way out I stepped on squishy fruit.

ANN GRANT

*My world opened up when I sat through Paul Muni and Luise Rainer in 'The
Good Earth'. It was a Thursday and the day before pay-day. The hall was empty
but I stuck it out and learned that life was hard for the Chinese as it was for all of
us then – it was hard raising 4d to get in.*

MATT BYRNE

There was no question that Hollywood provided what was desired.

*I never really liked British films. They reflected our own lives too much. The actors
dressed like us; the houses were similar to our own. There was no escapism. The
American films offered glamour and excitement, sheer fantasy – ordinary people
had lovely clothes and hairstyles, and lived in beautiful houses.*

CHRISTINE PAUL

*In the 1930s, British films did not make much of an impression
on us working-class people. The people on the screen seemed always to be
dressed in bow-ties, dickies and evening dress. Their language
was so la-di-dah, we thought they came from another world.
But we were very impressed with American productions.
We believed that was their way of life. Swimming pools,
College kids, all with cars. We got a series of families
from Hollywood. At home they looked so happy and rich,
no problems at all. I now know different. Those hero
fellows were not quite what they portrayed.*

WALTER WATT

*The pictures were a dream world for me, where
everyone was beautiful and handsome, no one went
to the toilet and babies were made with a kiss.*

HILDA THOMSON

33

STAND UP AND CHEER:
CHILDHOOD MEMORIES

For most of the early years of cinema there was no special product for children. They simply watched at matinées (much more cheaply) what their elders watched in the evening. In the 1920s few films were reckoned unsuitable, so it was a constant stream of Pickford, and serials with or without Pearl White, Chaplin, Rin Tin Tin, Tom Mix and his cowboy buddies.

One of the great mysteries of cinema in Scotland is the jeely jar. Were jam jars really accepted as entry to the pictures?

At the Palladium and the BB Picture House, the children used to get in to the Saturday matinée for a jam jar. If the children had a two pound jar, they got a pound back.

CATHERINE JARVIS

As for the story about jam jars, in those days you got money back if you returned your empty jam jars to the shop, so you took the jars to the shop to get your money to go to the pictures.

JOHN FINNIE

QUEUING FOR THE 'TEA SHOW', ENTRY WITH A QUARTER OF TEA, AT THE PALACE KINEMA, DUNFERMLINE. (SCOTTISH FILM AND TELEVISION ARCHIVE AT SCOTTISH SCREEN)

We went to the Embassy in Boswell Parkway to the Saturday matinée. I don't remember the films – 'Flash Gordon' rings a bell. We paid part of the entrance fee with jam jars.

JUNE McDONALD

My father grew up in Partick in the 1930s and told of getting into the pictures in Glasgow for the price of an empty jam jar. My mother usually disputed his story, but he held firm in his recollection, perhaps conceding that it may have been two jam jars that got him into a matinée.

COLIN CROMBIE

Our Saturday afternoons were spent at Bellshill picture house. No, we didn't get admittance with a jam jar, but my friend Bridget never had a penny for the pictures so we had to run to Liptons grocers shop with an empty jam jar so that she could get her entry money.

ROSINA MEIGHAN

Saturday matinées at the picture house in Thurso in the 1930s cost 3d, and that was not easily acquired – a loaf cost 4d. We boys took to collecting beer and lemonade bottles and jam jars, which realised the necessary at the pub and grocers.

J D MacDONALD

There used to be a cinema in Musselburgh called the Pavilion which held matinées on a Monday – and the price of admission was either lemonade bottles or jam jars.

JIM DUNSMORE

I'm sure I remember getting in by the side entrance at the Palace, Leith – with a jam jar.

GEORGINA MacGILLIVRAY

No cinema workers and no harassed cashiers with jars in their hands have come forward to back up the story. Yet there are Scots who are adamant they remember. Whatever the payment, for this child in Aberdeen going to the pictures was a very big deal indeed:

CHARLES OAKLEY'S SCOTTISH CINEMA AUDIENCE, 1946. (ABOVE)

I had no idea what moving pictures would be like. We entered the hall full of wooden seats; the curtains were closed; the noise of shouting was enormous. The ushers (or 'checkers' as we called them) were doing their best to bring us under control. I think some of them were sergeant majors from the Great War – they nearly all had ribbons on their chests. I sat there a bit confused about what was about to happen, when suddenly a beam of light appeared from away up high at the back of the hall. On the curtains was a Union Jack, something about news I was told, as I couldn't read. I thought the curtains were transparent until they opened and there was this picture with music coming from it. I can't remember the news in 1929 but I was really fascinated by that image. I kept looking up at that mysterious beam of light coming from a little window in the wall. Kids around me were shouting 'goodie' or 'baddie' – that meant nothing to me, but I joined in the fun. The worst bit was when a checker came round with that antiseptic spray, a massive brass pump. If you were at the end seat near the passageway you got a quite a drench and smelt like a hospital. I knew, as I had not long had my tonsils out.

WALTER WATT

For most young audiences in those days, cinema was a journey West of the Pecos and Across the Wide Missouri.

Nothing could supplant the Western, or the magic of loping home across the park with the streets transformed into badlands, and the dust of a wagon train on the horizon watched by a lone Indian on a pinto pony.

JENNI CALDER

The Theatre Royal, Coatbridge, was known as The Ranch due to all the Westerns it showed. They were all crystal clear – the 'goodies' were clean-shaven and rode white horses; the 'baddies' usually sported a three-week growth, with horses

as black as their hats (and their hearts). There was always a hard-bitten
saloon gal with a heart of gold, and goodness triumphed over villainy in every
last reel. Roy Rogers and Gene Autry weren't real cowboys though – not like
John Wayne and Gary Cooper – they were too clean-cut, talked to their
horses, and sang in the saddle.

JOE McDONAGH

The cowboys then are now forgotten – William S Hart, Tom Mix, Buck Jones,
William Farnum. In the old days the cowboy used to tie his horse with a secure
knot – now they wrap the rein round the bar casually with a loop that would hold
nothing. Maybe that is because they are now so rich and don't recognise
the value of a horse. In the old days they did.

ALBERT CURRAN

38

In Thurso, however, it was not only children who enjoyed the cowboy
antics …

The matinée was usually mobbed with screaming kids, but the front row more
often than not rapidly filled up with adult tinkers who went ballistic if any injun
threatened Tom Mix. Musicals and romantic films were of no interest at that time,
but a few years later we were all eyes. In a piece of one-upmanship the local message
boys on their bikes were the first to pick up and whistle the latest musical hits.

J D MacDonald

John Wayne could, on occasion, attract an unlikely audience:

There wis this auld farmer frae Mintlaw fa' went intae Aberdeen tae the Mart one Friday. He bought some ewes and saw them awa' onto the floatie. His wife was awfy fond o' ducks and geese and while he was there he bought her a very bonny duck as a wee present (he wis a nice auld boy – nae wan o' yer uncouth Buchan chiels). Now, he had a wee bit of time on his hauns so he thocht he would go and have a look at fit was gan on in Union Street. Mind I said he had some time afore he had tae heid back to Mintlaw, so as he passed the Gaumont he thocht he would jist gang in tae see the matinée. (I canna mind fit wis on at the time – but it micht hae been a Western. The loon frae Ellon said the auld yin was fair partial to Westerns.)

Onyway, the auld farmer kent he widna get in tae the flicks wi' the duck, so he thocht he wid jist pit it inside his jaicket. This worked – oh he wis fair tickled at the ruse – and he made his way inside and settled doon tae enjoy the film. (I mind noo – it wis 'Rio Bravo' wi' Big John Wayne and Walter 'Stumpy' Brennan.) Everything gaed fine until about half-way through, when the duck started tae get a bit restless and poked its heid and neck through the auld yin's jacket .... Weel now, there wis a wee lad and his maw sitting in the same row next tae the fairmer. The wee laddie turns to his maw and whispers, 'Maw, Maw there's yin o' thon flashers sittin' next tae me'.

The mither hisses back, 'I've telt ye afore – its best to ignore them and they'll no bother ye'. The wee laddie replies, 'I wid, Maw, but this yin's eating ma popcorn!'

T C

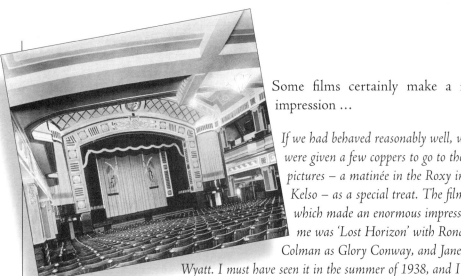

Some films certainly make a major impression ...

THE RITZ, EDINBURGH. (SCOTTISH FILM AND TELEVISION ARCHIVE AT SCOTTISH SCREEN)

If we had behaved reasonably well, we were given a few coppers to go to the pictures – a matinée in the Roxy in Kelso – as a special treat. The film which made an enormous impression on me was 'Lost Horizon' with Ronald Colman as Glory Conway, and Jane Wyatt. I must have seen it in the summer of 1938, and I became fascinated by the concept of a Utopian valley Shangri-La hidden in the Himalayas. Conway became my hero (perhaps my having the same first name as Colman helped), and Shangri-La became my target. No amount of questioning of how that grand piano was manhandled over that pass diminished my ideal!

I don't think the film made anything like the same impact on my friends, but the image of that pass and the ideal of Shangri-La stayed with me, and it became my ambition to get to Tibet – to see if I could find my Shangri-La.

It was not until I was 50 years old that I signed on for a trekking expedition round the Annapurna range in the Himalayas. The trek took us through a pass to the north side of the Himalaya range, and we reached a high tundra plateau only a couple of miles from the Tibetan frontier. I did not see Shangri-La, but I was invited into a very small, dark, shabby but strangely impressive monastery. The music and chanting sent shivers up my spine, and the monks were as courteous and welcoming to me and my party as the monks in 'Lost Horizon' had been to Conway and his.

RONNIE CRAMOND

And some do not, as page 41 reveals.

YOUNG LOVE

Top
Without Romberg's melodies Ramon Novarro and Norma Shearer still conjured up lyrical romance in 'The Student Prince' in 1927.

Left
You've heard him sing, now read the book! Jolson in the title role and Davey Lee as Sonny Boy, 1928. (Bill Douglas Centre for the History of Cinema and Popular Culture)

SINGING FOOL
by
Hubert Dail

ILLUSTRATED
EDITION

AL JOLSON

Left
Everybody sang when the Talkies came, whether they had voices or not, including America's sweethearts – Gaynor and Farrell, 1929.

Below
Today she is a sweet lady in her 70s, reassuringly little changed from the child the world loved in the 1930s.

Left
Dorothy and Toto get caught in a twister – when they wake in Technicolor, it sure ain't Kansas. 17 year-old Judy Garland becomes a star, 1939.

Below
Brunette Margarita Cansino transformed from Latin dancer into flame-haired love goddess – the enigmatic Rita Hayworth as 'Gilda' in 1946.

Left
On screen she might be Mata Hari, but at home her famous *visage* could store shortbread – the incomparable Garbo. (Bill Douglas Centre for the History of Cinema and Popular Culture)

Below
Forbidden romance in an exotic locale – what CinemaScope and Ava Gardner were invented for, 1956.

CONFESSION! Ava Gardner, half-caste, admits her love for Stewart Granger, and confesses to murder.

M-G-M presents "BHOWANI JUNCTION" in CinemaScope and Color

7

Property of National Screen Service Corp. Licensed for display only in connection with the exhibition of this picture at your theatre. Must be returned immediately thereafter.

55-473

COUNTRY OF ORIGIN U. S. A.

Copyright 1956 Loew's Incorporated

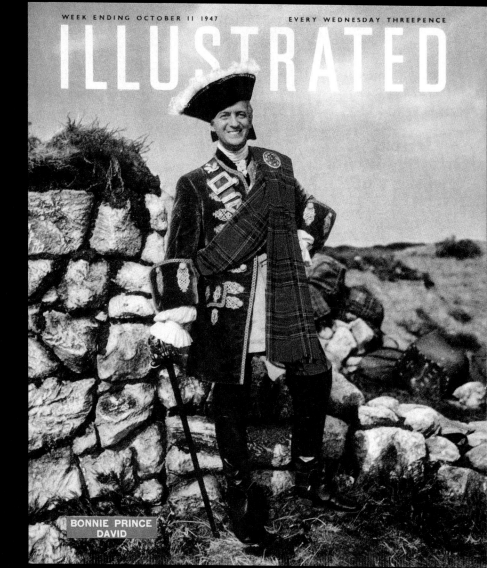

ILLUSTRATED

BONNIE PRINCE DAVID

Bonnie Prince David cover. As our darling Charlie, David Niven recklessly tackles the heather, the wig, and the myth in 1948.

M-G-M PRESENTS

"BRIGADOON"

STARRING

GENE KELLY
VAN JOHNSON
CYD CHARISSE

WITH

ELAINE STEWART

BARRY JONES · ALBERT SHARPE

New entertainment magic from the same producer ... emy Award-winning "An American in Paris"!

EALING STUDIOS PRESENT

BASIL RADFORD & JOAN GREENWOOD in

A HIGHLAND FLING ON A TIGHT LITTLE ISLAND

WHISKY GALORE!

FROM THE NOVEL BY COMPTON MACKENZIE

with JAMES ROBERTSON JUSTICE and GORDON JACKSON

A MICHAEL BALCON PRODUCTION
DIRECTED BY ALEXANDER MACKENDRICK
SCREENPLAY BY COMPTON MACKENZIE & ANGUS MACPHAIL

Above
When he stumbled on his enchanted glen Gene Kelly found the locals tall, dark and ballet-trained, 1954.

Left
Photogenic Barra, a droll cast, and a cargo-load of high spirits brighten Compton Mackenzie's island yarn in 1948. (Scottish Life Archive)

Art deco splendour on Sauchiehall Street – the La Scala, Glasgow. (Scottish Film and Television Archive at Scottish Screen)

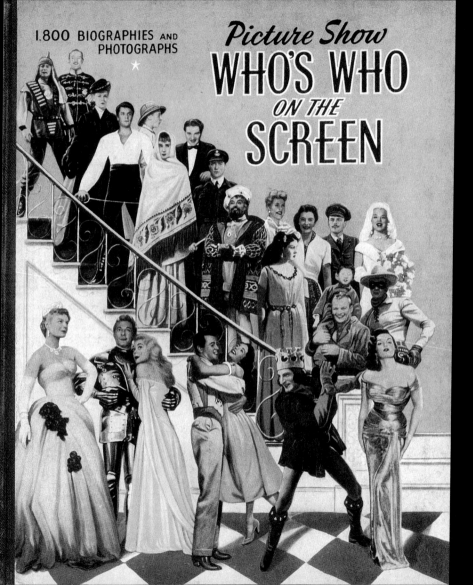

1.800 BIOGRAPHIES AND PHOTOGRAPHS

Picture Show
WHO'S WHO
ON THE
SCREEN

Anna Neagle takes first place while Liberace looks on – a fantasy photocall in 1956 brings out the stars, major and minor.

My first time at the pictures was when my mother took me to an afternoon showing of 'Gone With The Wind'. I was two-and-a-half years old. I remember running up and down the balcony aisle stairs while she plied me with sweets and watched the film.

Pictures were the family's main source of entertainment, for example in 1950:

Sunday   Day of rest
Monday   Pictures 6.30 pm
Tuesday   Pictures 4 pm
Wednesday   At home
Thursday   Pictures 4 pm
Friday   Tin bath night at home
Saturday am   Odeon Anniesland to see 'Flash Gordon'
Saturday pm   Family at pictures. Rounded off by a poke of chips and 'Mars' bar, shared by three of us.

HILDA THOMSON

For children, ghosts are ghosts – even if comics or great actors are involved.

Every other summer we spent in Cullen on the Banffshire coast.
The movies came to Cullen on a Saturday night. The village hall was only five minutes from the house we rented and my brother and I were allowed to go. That's where I met Laurel and Hardy, Abbot and Costello, and Arthur Askey. One night the film was 'The Ghost Train', probably the 1941 remake.

EVEN SCREEN STARS
HAD TO COPE WITH
RATIONING.
(PICTURE SHOW ANNUAL, 1949)

Alan and I were despatched off, leaving my parents lingering over their tea. We sat on benches and the projector clicked and hiccupped. All I can remember about the film is that I was terrified. I edged off the hard seat, gradually retreated to the back *of the hall, and finally ran out the door and back home. But having got home I couldn't bear the thought of missing the movie, so I crept back. But not for long. I raced home a second time, much to my parents' amusement, but again couldn't stay away. I remember slipping through the door, the flickering black and white at the far end of the hall, the erratic whirring of the projector somehow intensifying the hauntings on the screen.*

I must have been about eight when I experienced a screen haunting of a different kind. I was taken to see the Olivier film of 'Hamlet'. The deep gloom of the castle, the opening sequence on the battlements, the insubstantial but sonorous ghost … these images were my introduction to Shakespeare and ensured that he was a hit.

JENNI CALDER

But hiding was not always about horrors:

As children we'd hide under our seats seconds before the lights went up if we wanted to see the films again. Two things made this difficult: (a) the seat had to be held down in some ingenious way whilst you squatted underneath, and (b) the usher was up to your tricks!

GEORGE ANDERSON

My first visit to a proper cinema was to the North Star in Lerwick during World War II. For us then, a 25-mile trip to Lerwick was almost as rare as a trip overseas nowadays. I was still quite a young child. Unfortunately for me the film contained German soldiers (most of whom seemed to shout fiercely), and I was so scared that I covered my eyes with a Beano and only occasionally peeped out from behind its pages.

HECTOR JOHNSON

The thing I remember about Gourock Picture House was its front was on Kempock Place and its back on Adelaide Street, where there was a back door with a letterbox. If you looked through, you could see the back of the screen and get a preview of the picture – till your mates shouted it was their turn or the management cottoned on and you got hunted. The Central Picture House in West Blackhall Street in Greenock had a coal fire in the vestibule, and there was one in Rue End Street where you could get your feet wet in the front row at certain states of high tide.

My mother was always apprehensive about me going to the pictures on my own. I always got a lecture about what to do in case of fire – this was because of what had happened in Paisley at a cinema where a number of children had lost their lives.

CORNELIUS COWARD

I can recall 'Bambi' and the excitement of my first colour film. Television wasn't a household commodity then and this may account for the strong impact it had on me – the cold pies which my mother distributed during the performance have also lingered as a memory!

DOROTHY LAING

THE NORTH STAR, LERWICK, SHETLAND, SCOTLAND'S MOST NORTHERLY SCREEN. (SHETLAND MUSEUM) (LEFT)

My earliest memories of the cinema in Edinburgh during the last war were not happy ones. I was taken to see 'Dumbo', but instead of being captivated by Disney's colourful cartoon, I was in tears because the baby elephant had lost his Mummy, and I had to be taken out of the cinema. 'The Wizard Of Oz' was equally upsetting, although as I was a little older by then, I gritted my teeth and sat through the whole film – but all the time I was desperate for Dorothy to get back to her home. I wasn't too keen on Snow White either.

LOUISE BOREHAM

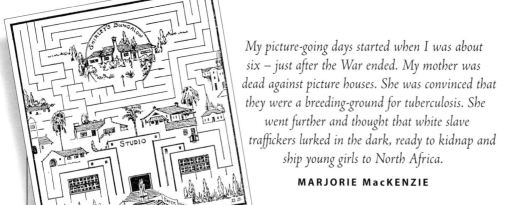

My picture-going days started when I was about six – just after the War ended. My mother was dead against picture houses. She was convinced that they were a breeding-ground for tuberculosis. She went further and thought that white slave traffickers lurked in the dark, ready to kidnap and ship young girls to North Africa.

MARJORIE MacKENZIE

There were three cinemas within walking distance of my home and a fourth which involved crossing a main road. We thought this was the reason why we were forbidden to go there. This particular day, I reneged on going to see yet another cowboy film with the boys, and suggested we cross the road and go to the Scotia cinema showing 'The Four Feathers'. It only cost a penny; the other cinemas tuppence – this meant we had a penny each to spend on sweets. Arriving home for tea, all seated at the table, Mum asked if we had enjoyed the film, who was in it, and what was it about? We thought we did a good job explaining the (any) cowboy film, but it didn't cut the mustard with Mum, who accused us of lying and packed us off to bed early without supper.

How did she know? It was practice then to spray the cinemas with air-freshener – usually very pungent floral ones, but the Scotia had an obnoxious disinfectant which had us all sneezing. It also stuck to our clothes.

MABEL CUNNINGHAM

The cinema could also lure adults – with disastrous consequences, as Mrs Muir and her little daughter found one cold night …

SHE WAS 'CURLY TOP', 'DIMPLES' AND 'HEIDI' BUT ALWAYS SHIRLEY TEMPLE; AND FIND YOUR WAY ROUND THE FOX LOT (LEFT) – FROM SHIRLEY TEMPLE'S ANNUAL.

Larkhall had three picture houses: the Empire, the Regal and the Flea Pit, which no self-respecting cinema-goer would be seen going into. Well, Mum wanted to see the film on in the Flea Pit, and took me with her without telling my policeman father, who was on duty that night, exactly where we were going.
It was wintertime, very frosty.

When we got home there was water cascading downstairs like a waterfall – we had had a burst pipe in the loft. The neighbours had broken into the house when they spotted water pouring out of the front door. They knew we had gone to the cinema, so had had an announcement made in the Regal and the Empire – no one thought about the Flea Pit!

MARION MURRAY

What was the film ? I hope it was 'The Rains Came'.
Cinema could be of the educational variety in Fife; worth impersonation:

When I was training to be a French polisher there was a picture to be shown at the Palladium about venereal disease. You had to be 16 to get in, and I was only 14. The older girls said, 'Come on, we'll get you in'. When we got to the cash desk, the cashier asked if I was 16. Two girls, one on each side of me, helped me off my feet, and I said I was 16. I got to see it.

CATHERINE JARVIS

If my mother didn't have money we didn't get to the cinema, end of story, but others were much more enterprising, like the lad who would wear his father's coat – and clinging to him like a monkey would be his young brother. After buying the ticket, they would go to the toilet where the young brother would stay until his brother's ticket was checked. Then he would return to the toilet and give the wee brother his half, which the usherette duly checked and allowed him to enter. Then the big brother would return but the usherette never challenged him as she had seen him go out. Another ploy was for the tallest member of the family to buy a ticket, get as far as the usherette, change his mind, go to the toilet and pass his ticket out to another member of the family. After having the ticket checked, he would go to the toilet and give his half to the first member of the family, then he would return – and because the usherette had seen him leave she didn't check his ticket – and the other member would emerge with his original ticket. We were really desperate wee people; we lived for the cinema and all its fantasy.

ANN YOUNG

The cinema circuits realised that they could tap into a special juvenile market and create a lot of goodwill on a Saturday morning by starting up clubs. Mickey Mouse had one, so did Gaumont-British (Shirley Temple even was their President), and so did ABC. It was the home of noise and club songs, thrilling serials and cowboys riding the range.

Every Saturday morning they had the children's club. There were always cartoons and a serial. At the end the hero (someone like Flash Gordon) fell (or was pushed) over a cliff. You could hardly wait till the next week! Only to find out he was saved before he got anywhere near the edge. But we still marvelled at his courage.

JIMMY NIVEN

In the early 1950s, together with my younger brother, I joined the cinema club for kids, the ABC minors in the Embassy Cinema in East Pilton. The films were shown on Saturday mornings and were preceded by an enthusiastic, if not altogether tuneful, rendering from hundreds of throats of the club song, sung to the tune of a

ALL THE SATURDAY MORNING FAVOURITES GATHER FOR A BIRTHDAY CELEBRATION. (BILL DOUGLAS CENTRE FOR THE HISTORY OF CINEMA AND POPULAR CULTURE)

military march. We were a noisy lot but reasonably well-behaved, though club-lore was to avoid sitting in the stalls immediately below the overhang of the balcony, from whence empty ice-cream tubs and other assorted cartons might descend.

IAN STUART

We are the boys and girls well known as
Minors of the ABC,
And every Saturday all line up
To see the films we like and shout aloud with glee.
We like to laugh and have our sing-song
Just a happy crowd are we-e
We're all pals together
We're Minors of the ABC.

As well as showing films, they had competitions. Once I won a box of Cadbury's chocolates in a pink box. I ate them on my mile-walk home, but preserved the box to show the family. One Friday, through the night, I took appendicitis and was bawling and protesting at having to go to hospital right away, wanting to wait till Saturday afternoon so that I would not miss the Minors. My friend Anna won the Tarzan-call competition, beating all the boys.

HAZEL GALLOWAY

On those Saturdays there was a stampede at the end to avoid having to sing 'God Save The King'. If you got caught leaving while it was being played, you were made to stand right where you were and look respectful till it had finished.

BILL COOPER

Those were the days when a child could go to the community's picture house alone.

When I was about six or seven, I recall watching a Shirley Temple film – the one where she sang 'On The Good Ship Lollipop'. I fell asleep during that film and must have slept off-and-on for about four hours. My mother had wondered where I was and had come down to the cinema. The management scratched a notice on a bit of smoked glass – 'Dickie Alexander please go to the kiosk' – and projected it onto the screen. I happened to be awake at that point and went home.

DICKIE ALEXANDER

And there were some great role models. Private lives of famous stars were private in 1938, and a great athlete could be admired, tights and all.

Films like 'The Adventures Of Robin Hood' featuring Errol Flynn and Basil Rathbone led us children into visiting the local joiners for timber slats for our swords and bamboo cane for bows and arrows. The tenement entrance was propped up with wood right through to the back court, and these high and criss-cross timbers became our Sherwood Forest.

FREDDIE MARTIN

We lived in a world of make-believe, fantasy and envy. As children we played games in gardens, sheds, and our homes. Our imaginations led us to make up plays. We had concerts on wet days in a garage. We borrowed high-heeled shoes, evening dresses, hats, stoles, furs and make-up from our mothers. Rouge and red, red lipstick which we plastered on. We were Hollywood actresses.

LUCINDA ALLAN

Scotland's attitude to pleasure was not always clear, and in some parts of the country the glamour of Hollywood was not to be trusted:

When the Stornoway Playhouse was being built in the early 1930s, people were grateful for the work it created – but there were reservations, and for some such a thing as cinema was frowned upon. It was even said that the Brahan Seer had predicted such a place. It was, he said, to be burnt down with a great loss of life. Only one small fair-haired child would be saved. Silent pictures had been shown at Will Mack's Picture House, but the Playhouse promised luxury. When I first got to go, after much pleading with my parents, I entered with a mixture of fear and excitement because of the oft-repeated prophecy.

CHRISTINA MacLEAN

Outside towns in the north, cinema came to villagers through the Highlands and Islands Film Guild setting up in a local school or hall. Locations were not so grand, but the experience often lively and unpredictable.

On Yell, my memories are not so much about the films themselves, more about the cold! There was no electricity and no heating in the public hall – so it was a case of wrapping up well before you went. And also wrapped up (in a paper) to take with you, was a hot brick straight out of the Rayburn oven. My brother used to nip home during the pictures for a drink or a pee or to get his hot water bottle refilled. Me and my brothers and sisters used to go aroond the banks looking for washed-up lemonade bottles to put to the shop for a refund so that we could get to the pictures on a Saturday night. You got 3d for a 'Hays' lemonade bottle, but best of all was a 'Lucozade' one – 6d for that!

JEANETTE NOWAK

We used to go to the pictures at a small village hall in Kemnay about 15 miles north of Aberdeen. This was the 1950s. It was next to the chippie – they did a good trade on the night the pictures came, usually a Tuesday. It was the highlight of the week – we walked five miles there and five miles back; some biked ….

There was always a queue to get the best seats at the front, away from the noise of the projector which made a click, click, click *sound. It didn't seem to bother me, I was so engrossed in the film. That was until the film broke or the speed slowed down on a whim – then the shouting started – chips and papers were thrown. Then, as soon as the film started, quiet again.*

STUART REID

In around 1950, a mobile cinema came on the scene in Lewis. They set up in the village schools about once a fortnight, and it was just wonderful, regardless of the many breakdowns or the long walk in winter. The magic of the big screen could not be spoilt. If we really enjoyed a certain film and we could wangle another half crown out of our parents, we could go and see it in the neighbouring village too. Ah, happy days.

G C

Here are memories of grander occasions in the Highlands of the 1930s, when the local hotelier made a great trip to town in a fine car:

The highlight of the school holidays was when my grandmother and great aunt decided they would like to see a film in Inverness, over 30 miles away. What a performance before we even started out, as with no heating in the car in the early '30s, hot water bottles had to be filled and rugs wrapped round us for the journey in midwinter. What I really enjoyed was the café in one Inverness cinema. We sat in an alcove watching the film. 'Rin Tin Tin', I remember, and films set on the North-west Frontier, with troops fighting in the Khyber Pass.

LUCINDA ALLAN

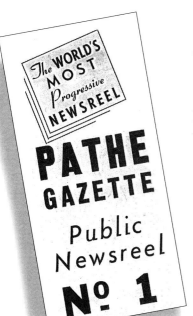

The WORLD'S MOST Progressive NEWSREEL

PATHE GAZETTE Public Newsreel Nº 1

Even at a young age, this Fifer noted the conflicting glamour and drabness of a night out:

The projector light was fascinating in the darkness as it constantly changed its tone working at the screen – some of the bolder sports threw up pieces of silver paper and these twinkled like stars for an instant before falling. The most dangerous seats in the cinema were under the balcony.

In the darkness, cigarette ends, apple runts and other missiles would descend with sudden shock on the recipients below. After all the fun, glamour and excitement of the programme, what a difference when the lights went on at the close. The place had a musty, sweaty odour, the curtains looked faded and dowdy, litter lay every-where, and you were in danger of being crushed as the crowds jostled and fought to get out.

JIM DOUGLAS

The Monsignor was wonderful on wet afternoons – some people remember their childhoods as taking place in perpetual sunshine, I understand, but lots of mine took place indoors on wet afternoons, when you could watch cartoons by the hour and eat choc-ices. And when you came out, it was still light. Amazing.

I had to be taken out of 'Bambi' during the forest fire. Never found out what happened at the end. By the time I was taken to see 'Snow White', I was brave enough to sit through it – but only by keeping my eyes shut all the time the witch was making her eat the apple. I think I was more scared of the telling-off I would get from my mother if I had to be taken out than I was of the witch, but it was close.

HELEN McCORRY

An old man across the road from us once gave me a very good projector and some old films. Friends and my sisters would crowd our bedroom for a film-show. There was no screen so the projector would be focussed on a wall. The other thing missing was a container for the light bulb, which had to be a 250 watt or so. I made one out of a dried milk tin with a hole punched in one end for the light and a hole in the lid for the cable. How someone didn't get electrocuted, I don't know! The tin would become unbearably hot and we would hold it with a wet cloth to keep it cool. I turned the handle by hand quickly while the steam rose from the tin. We stopped from time to time to allow the tin to cool down, and on putting on the light, would often discover yards and yards of film on the floor. A friend was an apprentice operator in the Gothenburg and he gave me a load of cuttings from the feature films. On the bedroom wall we were then able to show stills of great stars sometimes; their heads much bigger than lifesize. It seemed a great achievement in a small bedroom watching Tarzan of the Apes gaze down from the trees above the bed.

JIM DOUGLAS

53

During summer holidays I stayed with an aunt and uncle in Duns. This meant great freedom. The Regal was up Easter Street just yards from the house. Wonderful, I could go twice a week. As I walked home after 'The Hound Of The Baskervilles' there, I thought of those hounds – and when I was tucked up in bed, after my cousin had put the Dinky curlers in my hair, I could not sleep a wink. I kept keeking out from below the sheets at every sound – even the clip, clip of folks walking on the pavement seemed menacing. And there was the pain of the curlers in my hair.

MARGARET LAVERICK

What cinema did was fire the imagination.

Being the youngest of the family, I wasn't allowed to go to the pictures as often as my brother and sisters. But hearing about them could be almost as good. After tea my brother and sister would see if they had enough money, and if they did they would go to the second house. Next night we'd all gather round the fireside. The kettle was always on the boil at the side of the range, and Mother would get out the bread and toasting fork, and we would have a plate of buttered toast and cups of tea. My brother would tell us word for word about the film he'd seen the previous night. If he dared to leave any out, my sister would help out. The rest of us would sit silent, spellbound as if we'd been there ourselves.

CHRISTINE PAUL

AN AUDIENCE ON STRONSAY, ORKNEY, ENJOY ABBOT AND COSTELLO, PROBABLY CHRISTMAS 1952. (SCOTTISH LIFE ARCHIVE)

54

The Regal

Amang waves tae split Atlas
Ah mairched on Rome
Defeated Napoleon
Took refuge wi Swiss Family Robinson.
The Regal cinema
Jist a skimmer awa fae the sea
Wis a hangar loadit wi planes
Aff tae the ootside an history.

Homer, The Aeneid –
Auld Reekie
Wir, as yet mony
Dimensions awa.

ANDREW McNEIL

ALL THIS AND HEAVEN TOO:
COURTING AND WINCHING

The great love teams were not always what they seemed, but Gaynor and Farrell, Hayworth and Ford, and Wyman and Hudson, were an encouragement to all those Scots out there in the stalls and the balcony. Never mind the romance on the screen – the cinema provided an important social function as the approved way for couples to explore their compatability. Encounters could be genteel or, given the restraints of the setting and the era, a bit more passionate. Whatever the intentions or outcome, it was the hopeful male who was required to pay for the treat.

Appreciating their market one of the biggest cinema managements in Scotland, Green's, introduced luxurious double seats for couples. That was the place to go if you were feeling flush.

My first date with my future husband was 'Gone With The Wind' in Green's Playhouse, Glasgow. That was a real adventure. To impress me he had booked golden divans right at the front of the balcony. I had on a new pair of high-heeled shoes and as I started to walk down I tripped and went sliding down the passage on my bottom. So much for a dignified entry.

MEGAN CATHCART

In those memorable days I was, on occasion, taken by a boyfriend to the best seats in Green's Playhouse – nicknamed the 'Golden Dive-ins' for apparent reason. I sank straight into the deep plush soft golden-padded cushions where, even between cuddling sessions, I was unable to see over the balcony. Missed 'A Star Is Born' and 'Gone With The Wind'. Wished I'd been taller.

ANNA MacDONALD

WE LOVED SCARLETT, SO DID RHETT, BUT SHE LOVED ASHLEY, AND HE LOVED MELANIE. STILL THE BEST-REMEMBERED FILM OF ALL, YEARS AFTER ITS 1939 DEBUT.

The film did not matter as long as you shared that special opportunity to smooch. It was the place for courting couples. Poor lads – they paid for us both in those days, and got very little in return. The constant comings and goings with the torches of the usherettes precluded any shenanigans. Nor were any portrayed on the screen. If you had not experienced sex in real life then all was left to your imagination.

ELSPETH BEATON

Films were not a good place to learn the facts of life – there were far too many chintzy rooms with the likes of Cary Grant and Irene Dunne in separate beds. Even Tarzan and Jane, who obviously were living up a tree in sin, had to find a son in a plane crash rather than let nature takes its course. From a male point of view sometimes there were confectionery matters to be dealt with, and of course it was not a good idea to compete with a screen idol.

The Picture House – labelled 'The Auld High Street' – was sedate, with posh, deep carpeting wall-to-wall; ideal for one's first dates, where the girl assessed if you were superior to your menial (temporary) day-to-day activity. A cinema where she feared rustling the wrappers in the (heavens!) one pound box of 'Terry's All Gold' – which, costing five shillings, made a second date problematic. When courting my late wife there was a wonderful sense of (disguised) relief when after the third box of 'All Gold' she said I was too kind, and not to spend so much. What a girl.

Funny how we both found we loved mixed balls, 4d a quarter, and Mrs Caldwell's fish and chips, next to the cheaper Alex Cinema. Two fish suppers and a bottle of kola (two glasses) – a shilling. What a splendid girl. We became engaged. The Alex became our cinema and the only jarring moments were my sweetheart's apparent crush on Gary Cooper, and her failure to accept my appreciation of the skills of Myrna Loy.

ALBERT BURNAP

Cinemas at the end of the 1940s were great value. The ticket would cost anything between sixpence and one shilling and thruppence. So you could see how a young man of the day could take his girl out, and after the show, afford to buy a slap-up meal in the chip shop, take her home in a taxi, and still have enough to buy a packet of fags – all this for less than ten shillings! The only snag, of course, was that our weekly pay at this time was something like 45 shillings!

JOHN WILLIAMSON

It was important to get the dress code worked out in advance, especially if the location was one of Edinburgh's finest.

It was to the Regal I took my very first and – as far as that young lady was concerned – last date. The trouble was that even though I had raked up enough money to treat her to the circle, I turned up in shorts. At my school they were still wearing shorts in sixth year if they felt like it – but I think my companion almost died of shame. When we parted that evening, it was forever.

JIM BRUNTON

Sometimes young women simply did not appreciate local talent:

My hero was Gene Kelly. I grant you Astaire was good, especially in white tie and tails, but Kelly seemed to have a wider range and was better looking. Besides, it was Kelly who usually finished up with Cyd Charisse. The sight of her used to make my hormones leap about like anything, I can tell you – even today they manage a little shuffle. So Kelly was both my hero and my target. I invite this very pretty and very nice girl to see 'Singin' In The Rain'. While she enjoyed it, I was transported. We left the Ritz and walked up Townhead Street. Well – she walked, I danced. I did the pavement, gutter, pavement, gutter bit, I leapt on and off

garden walls, I twirled round a lamppost or two, and I sang beautifully the while. 'Do stop that. It's cold and I want to get home,' she said.

W GORDON WATSON

And sometimes great mysteries took place in the 'Gents'.

I had arranged to meet a young man of very recent acquaintance at a cinema showing 'Michael Strogoff' with Anton Walbrook. We met at the arranged time outside the Elephant at Shawlands Cross. He bought the tickets and spent his precious sweet coupons on a very small box of chocolates for me. From the bright lights of the foyer, the queue went through a swing door into the darkness, where an usherette took us away a few at a time. While awaiting our turn he touched me on the shoulder and pointed to the door marked 'Gents'. I was left alone in everyone else's way, so I sat on the aisle seat of the back stalls, where I could keep a watchful eye for his return. I never saw him again – ever. I enjoyed the film and ate my chocolates.

VALERIE SMITH

Some young men were on the bold side.

As for romantic drama, who could forget 'Now Voyager'? I particularly remember that one which I saw in The Rex, Cumbernauld Road, with a girl friend who, during the film, seemed to disappear from my side vision. When I turned my head I saw that a young man sitting on the other side of my friend had placed his arm around her and put her head on his shoulder. He was a complete stranger, and must have been carried away with the romantic film!

MAY DUNN

Or perhaps he simply felt that one of the great wartime weepies left her vulnerable? Others were more appreciated.

My first date with my future wife was to see Ava Gardner in 'The Barefoot Contessa' at the Playhouse in 1955. Afterwards she said that when I put my arm around her it felt different from other guys – she felt this was the real thing.

JAMES MANDERSON

The Astoria in Kittybrewster was a large one with an organ which rose from the depths, usherettes with trays of ice-cream, and those huge swagged drapes which parted to reveal the screen and which gave the whole auditorium an air of magical opulence, bathed in red and gold spotlights. I recall taking my girlfriend there in what must have been the late 1950s, to 'Mardi Gras' with Pat Boone. We were in the back of the balcony, and missed the bulk of the film due to courtship wrestling. When we got back to my girlfriend's home, her father asked me whether we had been 'yav'lin'. Not knowing what the dialect word meant I blushed, suspecting saucy connotations.

'Yavel' means to repeat something in the Doric. Film performances were continuous then and you could see the film programme round again if you wished. This was the allusion he was making. We had indeed been yav'lin.

DONALD McGILP

By the 1960s things were getting a bit more scientific for the young Edinburgh ladies of the time.

The pictures. That's where you did all your snogging. You had to fight to get into the back row. And you could snog right through the second feature.

JUNE ROWAN

I would go to the State in Leith on a Saturday night with three or four pals. The picture wasn't important – the main point was to be chatted up by the boys in the row behind. They would tap on our shoulders and the seating arrangements would change.

THELMA HUNTER

When I was about 15, I bunked off school, took off my tie and blazer (stuck them in a bag) and went to the Pooles Synod Hall with a rather dodgy boyfriend to see (rather underage) some B horror movie. I cannot remember seeing my first X-rated movie because I was snogging throughout. I do, however, remember the hard, wooden, uncomfortable seats which were arranged in almost vertical tiers. At this stage, going to the cinema predated youth clubs and was a place to meet interesting people and snog them.

EDITH PHILIP

There were gentler times too. Having spent years watching rural Americana on the screen, one Scot got to be Doris Day or Jeanne Crain for real.

When I immigrated to the United States there was something I was excited about experiencing that could only have come from movies that I had seen in Scotland. That first summer, a boy who pumped gas at the local gas station appeared at my sister's house to ask me to go to the movies. She lived in a small rural village in Vermont. I remember the white door with the dark fly-screen panels in the centre; he was on one side and I on the other. We talked through the screen. I never did open the door, nor did I go to the pictures with him – but I have always loved the whole image that it created in my mind, just like the movies.

MEG WALKER

And for many there were happy endings …

Before we got married, my boyfriend and I went to the pictures every Monday, Wednesday, Friday and Saturday night. Then some cinemas started showing films on Sundays. So sometimes we went then too. We had picnics in the back row. I'd bake fairy cakes and my boyfriend would spread out his white hanky and we would sit and eat the cakes. I brought small Scotch tomatoes and unshelled garden peas and hard-boiled eggs. The night we got engaged, we exchanged rings in the back row of the Picture Palace. Then we went home to tell my mother and father. It was Christmas Eve.

CHRISTINE PAUL

… And I hope it was snowing.
It's a wonderful life.

63

TOGETHER

by B. G. DeSYLVA
LEW BROWN and
RAY HENDERSON

*featured
in the motion picture*

Since You Went Away

A DAVID O. SELZNICK
PRODUCTION

starring

**CLAUDETTE COLBERT · JENNIFER JONES
SHIRLEY TEMPLE · JOSEPH COTTEN
LIONEL BARRYMORE · MONTY WOOLLEY**

Directed by
JOHN CROMWELL

Released through

1/-

CAMPBELL, CONNELLY
& CO., LTD.
10, DENMARK ST., LONDON, W.C.2

CRAWFORD MUSIC CORP., NEW YORK

SINCE YOU WENT AWAY:
THE WAR YEARS

Ironically the years of World War II were good ones for cinema, and for cinema-going. There may have been a shortage of resources in the studios – including the young leading men now in the Forces – but films played an important part in boosting morale. In 1939 cinemas in Scotland were briefly shut down, but the authorities swiftly reconsidered. Wartime spirits would be kept high by the cinema – by Greer Garson's nobility, Mickey Rooney's vitality, Bob Hope's jokes and Betty Grable's legs.

In October 1939 while waiting outside the Alhambra cinema on Leith Walk, my pal Ian Cameron called out 'Here comes a Jerry', and sure enough, without even a Gloster Gladiator in sight, a Junkers JU88 passed overhead on its way to bomb Leith docks. While everyone else was looking skywards at the low-flying bomber, Ian and I managed to move up the bed a bit and got in before the others to see 'Alexander's Ragtime Band'. While Ian and I were enjoying our love affair with Alice Faye and Tyrone Power, RAF pilots had downed Luftwaffe bombers into the Forth.

JAMES INGLIS

'THE FOUR MOST IMPORTANT WORDS SINCE "GONE WITH THE WIND",' WENT THE ADS. THE PERFECT AMERICAN FAMILY AT WAR, 1944.

Every cinema had its display of neon sadly blacked out during the war years, but soon put back in order when hostilities ceased. Some told a story. At Greens Brothers (whose empire included Europe's largest cinemas: the Playhouse, Glasgow and the Playhouse, Dundee, which had 4100 seats), the 'U' in 'Playhouse' was angled to one side with the caption 'We Want "U" In' supported by little neon elves.

G B MILLAR

Cinema-going could be a family outing for both entertainment and education.

When the War started in September 1939, our parents began taking the family of four children (eight to twelve years) to the pictures at least twice a week. There were three cinemas within walking distance of our home in Glasgow. The programme was continuous so you could walk in at any time. When the part of the film you came in at came round again, that's when you left.

For sixpence per adult and thruppence per child, you would get a cartoon plus another short film like the Pete Smith specialities – they were mini-documentaries, and a favourite of mine. Then there was 'Pathe News' – of particular interest to our parents as it was the only visual information on the War around in those pre-television days. Then we saw the B film – usually a cowboy with Gene Autry or Roy Rogers. These were my brother's favourites. Next came the big picture. It could be a musical with Betty Grable and John Payne, a gangster picture with George Raft or Pat O'Brien, a war film with John Wayne, or a love story with Ingrid Bergman or Paulette Goddard. At the end of the feature, at about 10.30 pm, they would show a short of the Royal Family and play 'God Save The King'. Everyone in the cinema would stand. Well, nearly everyone – some people just walked out.

JOAN CONNELLY

Ending every programme was 'The King', a film lasting about a minute – just long enough for one verse of 'God Save The King'. Various versions were available: both black and white, and colour. Most utilised pictures of battleships, aeroplanes, brass bands, flags and of course HM the King. The rule was that everyone in the auditorium stood to attention while this was shown, and most did.

G B MILLAR

Working in the pictures in Glasgow during the War had its challenges …

One Monday morning we were informed that only one copy of the film had arrived for both the Coliseum and the Regal in Sauchiehall Street. One of the copies had been in a bombed cinema and the film was destroyed. Could we manage to have only one copy between the two cinemas? So we worked out that if the Regal started 20 minutes before us and went quickly, and we took our time, there was a chance we could get the film back and forth by taxi. All went well till the last bit of the evening. The Regal rang up and said they would send us the two last reels together. We had about five minutes left on the last reel we had, but the others had not arrived. So we rang up – they were on their way! But they did not arrive. We showed the newsreel again and apologised to the audience. We sent the doorman to see what had happened – the taxi was jammed between two tram cars on the corner of Sauchiehall Street and Renfield Street. They had managed to get the driver out by cutting open the roof, but the film was still in there. In the end the film did arrive and was duly shown, but all the staff that didn't live locally missed the last bus. It was a long walk home.

DICK HOLYOAK

But nothing could put off a young enthusiast …

I was enamoured of the movies – where one could be transported to another world – away from hearing sirens, running to air-raid shelters, carrying gas masks and making sure you had your ear-plugs in the

gas mask case. I remember the presentation being stopped for a minute as we heard the announcement of an air-raid warning; however the picture continued and we kept our seats.

Saturday morning – who would get the Fife Free Press first to see what was on the following week? Me! Naturally, on our way there we would want to have a 'sweet' during the performance, so we stopped at a small shop around the corner from Church Street on St Clair Street and, coupons in hand, bought out our allotted two ounces. I remember many times in the wartime in the winter and on ice, carefully treading my way with friends up Church Street after a night at the Rio, with a hand over an already-shaded torch (no lights on anywhere), but we had enjoyed a great double-feature with all the extras.

MARGARET MELDRUM

Most of film-going days on my own were during the War and the blackout. I was given 2/6 a week pocket money, and 2/6 to get national saving [sic] stamps at school. Some weeks I didn't buy that stamp – it was used for the pictures. I had a season ticket for the bus; Mum paid for my Picture Show and Picturegoer magazines, so all my pocket money went on going to the pictures, or on postage – as I used to write off for autographed photos of stars for my collection.

To get in, I usually paid 1/6, 1/9, 2/3 and only once 3/6, if there was nothing cheaper. I would queue on the pavement, and if it was an A-certificate film I would ask the adult in front of me, man or woman, if they would take my money and pay me in with them. I went into Edinburgh twice every week after my homework was completed, to the New Victoria, the Playhouse, the Palace and the

*New. How I wished I could dance like Rita, swim like Esther, or even skate
like Sonja Henie. If I missed the last bus from St Andrews Square, I had to catch
a tram to Liberton, then I had another mile or so to walk after that in the
pitch dark. I never gave it a thought, no fear at all.*

MARGARET LAVERICK

But sometimes it was all just too much.

*One night my sister and her boyfriend stood in the queue for over two hours
to see a Betty Grable picture. She saw the titles at the start, fell fast asleep and
woke to see the end credits. She had been called up for munitions and was
working shifts. I can still remember her bad mood when she came home
and told us how she'd missed the film.*

CHRISTINE PAUL

*During the War, the north-east of Scotland was bombed regularly by the
Luftwaffe; Aberdeen, Fraserburgh and Peterhead all being attacked. On one
occasion the film being shown at the Regal, Peterhead, was due for showing at
another northern venue the following day, but could not be uplifted by the transport
service because of the presence of an unexploded bomb – in the cinema. A house
across the street – and its occupants – had had an amazing escape, for the bomb
had a faulty tail-unit and, instead of going point-down after leaving the aircraft,
continued on its way down sideways. Reaching the ground, it first hit the roof of the
house, shifting some slates, then skidded across the street, mounted the pavement,
then the steps and on through the glass doors into the foyer – where it came to rest
alongside a pile of film transit boxes. A bomb disposal team did their duty and the
film arrived at its destination just in time for the evening performance.*

G B MILLAR

During the War we had to think carefully about which picture hall we went to. We usually tried to go to the one nearest to where we lived so that we had a chance of making it back home to be all together during the air-raid. Sometimes we went to the furthest one away as it was showing a great film. We'd hope and pray the siren didn't go. A notice would appear on the screen to let us know when the alert had sounded.

When I came home from school my mother would make the tea early, then fill a vacuum-flask with tea, and we'd hurry down-town to stand in the picture queue and keep a place for my sister who would come straight from work. It was quite common to see folk drinking tea and eating sandwiches in the queue. It was not uncommon to wait an hour or so, so the buskers who entertained outside the cinema were welcome. As the first house came out we'd look to see if the people had red eyes with crying. If they had, then we'd know it was a good picture. I used to put cold water on my eyes in the ladies' room – I hated coming out looking all red.

CHRISTINE PAUL

the **GRETA**

SURE
SWIFT
SAFE

6^D

HAIR REMOVING GLOVE

A marvellous advance, not a mere improvement but something really NEW—The Greta Hair Removing Glove. Entirely dispenses with razors, paste, or dangerous chemicals. A few minutes soothing massage and the hair disappears, leaving smooth, white skin. No odour, no mess, no irritation, or clogging of the pores. Be free from unwanted hair on legs and arms.

Send 7½d. in stamps to Greta Products, Dept. F.P., 6 Gordon Place, London, W.C.1, and the Greta Hair Removing Glove will be sent you post free.

I really sobbed throughout 'Lassie Come Home' and a man sitting near us kept offering me sweets to stop me crying. I managed to reassure him that despite the tears I was really enjoying it, sad bits and all.

MARY BETT

Wartime weepies were a staple. With the men away at war, Bette Davis and Irene Dunne had the field to themselves, till Greer Garson came along to show them.

Wednesday January 29th 1941
I am glad that I was well enough today after my flu, to go with Kay to see 'Pride And Prejudice' at the BB. It was the best film I have seen so far.

Saturday February 1st 1941
Kay and I went to the BB in Greenock and saw 'New Moon', with Jeanette MacDonald and Nelson Eddy. It was lovely and the singing was wonderful.

Saturday February 8th 1941
We went to see 'The Great Dictator' at the Regal. It was a waste of time!

Saturday March 8th 1941
Kay and I went to Greenock Palace. The film 'Boy Meets Girl', James Cagney and Pat O'Brien. It was a lot of nonsense but we did get a lot of laughs.

Saturday March 15th 1941
Pictures as usual, Kay and I went to the Regal and saw 'Rhythm Of The River', with Bing Crosby. It was great. I think he is a swell singer. Seeing this film cheered me up a lot after Thursday night. The sirens went at 9.30 pm and we didn't get the all-clear until 5.30 am on Friday morning. An eight-hour raid with lots of bombs dropped. It was terrifying. Bing Crosby's film was a great boost. I'll always remember it.

Saturday March 29th 1941
Kay's mumps are better now so we got back to the old routine. We saw Loretta Young and Melvyn Douglas in a very funny film.

Saturday April 26th 1941
Kay is officially a Wren now, so we haven't had so much time. We did get to see 'I Love You Again', with William Powell and Myrna Loy.

DRESS LIKE THE Stars

HOW TO REMODEL YOUR
WARDROBE ON THE LATEST FILM
STYLES WITHOUT COUPONS
EASY-TO-MAKE INSTRUCTIONS

It was great. We have had lots of air-raids recently and couldn't get out at night. Greenock was badly bombed on the 15th. Where will it all end? The pictures are about the only thing that helps one forget.

Tuesday May 6th 1941

We were going tonight to see Sabu in 'The Thief Of Bagdad', but after the terrible air-raid last night in Greenock it just wasn't possible.

MARGARET HOPKINS

HANDY HINTS FOR A WARTIME AUDIENCE, AND THE CHANCE TO LOOK LIKE MYRNA LOY. (BILL DOUGLAS CENTRE FOR THE HISTORY OF CINEMA AND POPULAR CULTURE)

For others on Clydeside, a night at the pictures ended in tragedy …

The 13th of March started off differently for us, as my mother had told us there was a Shirley Temple film on at the Regal picture house and she and my father were taking us there that night. As we normally only got to the matinée to see films, it was a rare treat to get out after tea and we were all very excited.

We went into the picture house and saw the shorter film and the news, and were well into the screening of the big film when the siren sounded. At that point, a lot of people went to get home. Some, including my father, who were on night fire-watch, had to go out. But mainly we were advised that everyone who could stay would be safer until the all-clear sounded. For a short time the film continued and then it was stopped. Just imagine how we children felt at having our Shirley Temple taken from us. That was a real tragedy. However, people began to get up onto the platform to sing and we all joined in. I think the reason the community singing was encouraged was to help drown out the noise of the planes.

But suddenly an incendiary bomb came through the roof and landed on the stage.
The wardens ran on with pumps and water hoses and everyone in the hall was
moved to the back underneath the balcony. That put paid to the singers,
who were a bit worn out by this time.

As the night wore on, we could hear all sorts of bombs falling and planes
flying low. It was quite frightening but there was a great sense of security as the
adults were keeping us all reassured. Every so often someone would shout in that
such and such an area had 'got it!' and I kept hoping my dad would come back.

It was early next morning when the all-clear went and we were allowed
out of the picture house and made our way home. No tram journey home this time.
The sight that met our eyes was hard to believe. The pavements and road were
either covered in debris from the tenements that were halved in two, or they were
covered in thousands of hoses as firemen and air-raid wardens were struggling to put
out massive fires. The tram cars were totally damaged and the tram lines were
curled up in the air. As we got to the other side of the road, we passed a pend. I
looked in and told my mum that a lot of people in there were sleeping as I saw rows
of legs sticking out from the tarpaulins. I was to know at a later date that they were
some of the many people who had lost their lives during that terrible night.

HELEN McNEIL

I will never forget a visit the family made to the Regal cinema around
1941 or 1942. We had seen a Cisco Kid exploit with Cesar Romero, which was
followed by a British Movietone news sequence, during the course of which a
German plane was shown being shot down over the sea. The commentator had no
sooner uttered the words 'One more of Jerry's aircraft comes to grief', when my
father got to his feet and shouted in anguish, 'My son was killed when his plane
crashed into the sea'. The reaction was futile, but understandable. It was the only

"Every girl should have a lovely Lux Complexion" says this charming young star

Veronica Lake

9 out of 10 Screen Stars use Lux Toilet Soap

occasion I remember my father showing his pent-up *feelings about the death of my brother Arthur, who was killed in action with the RAF in 1940. We left the cinema at that point. Following this incident I tended to go to the pictures on my own.*

GEORGE BAIRD

Most cinema-goers took it all in their stride.

The lights would go up, the manager in his tuxedo would appear on the stage announcing the sirens had sounded, when there was a bit of scramble to go out and get home. Latterly we got a bit blasé about the whole thing. Until one night when I'd gone on my own to the Waverley, waiting till the end of the show, walking home developed into a run when I realised that what I was hearing was shrapnel falling on the slates of the buildings.

STANFORD McNAUGHT

There are stories that 'Gone With The Wind' turned up in small towns by mistake when it was still a big city treat, but big attraction or not, the pictures were still the only place to go.

Cinema-going was at its peak during the War as the town was packed with troops who were training in the hills around the town. As well as rewinding the film during the shows, I had to control the queue at the door of the Town Hall. At 15, I was small for my age – just clearing five foot and with a slight build – and it was a daunting task to hold back all the soldiers, some of them commandos well over six foot. When the hall was full it could get a bit confrontational explaining to them there was no more room inside.

JOHN MURRAY

*During the War, the RAF was billeted next door to us and some of the
airmen would spend their free time in our house. One of the men was being posted
and asked me to go with him to see Marlene Dietrich in 'Destry Rides Again'. When
we got to the cinema he didn't have quite enough money to get us in, and I hadn't
brought my purse, but the girl at the cash desk let us in. Half-way through we decided
we didn't like it, so crept out guiltily – feeling glad we hadn't paid the full price.*

EIRA LANGLER

*During the War, a friend and I went out to celebrate his
commission in the RAF. We had a few drinks and then went to the pictures –
he was smartly turned-out in his new uniform. During the performance he had to
visit the loo, and returning to his seat and edging his away along the row, he realised
the new-fangled zip on his trousers was not secure, so he hastily pulled it up. From
the row in front, a howl of anguish. In those days hairstyles à la Veronica Lake
were very popular, and the long locks fell over the back of the seats. Hence,
disaster. One unfortunate lassie was now snarled up in his zip.*

*The film had to be halted, the lights put on, and a pair of scissors found to
free the pair. He was one very subdued officer rookie.*

ANTHONY ROBB

But when it did all come to an end, it was a time to forget about escapism
in the dark, pack up your troubles, and take to your feet.

*As a young girl I once went to the Odeon, Motherwell,
to see Frank Sinatra in a movie. Half-way through the lights went on
and the manager walked onto the stage and announced that it was VE day.
The whole place erupted into applause and everyone left, dancing out into the
street. No one saw the end of the film!*

ELIZABETH MAXWELL

BORIS KARLOFF IN NIGHT KEY WITH WARREN HULL
ALSO JEAN ROGERS IN THE WILDCATTER

TONIGHT AND EVERY NIGHT:
MAKING A LIVING

For some, of course, the cinema was not just an entertainment – it was a job.

Scotland had its share of enterprising exhibitors, independent circuits often with their origins in the touring fairground families of late Victorian days. There were the Kemps in Ayrshire, the Pooles in Edinburgh, the Donalds in Aberdeen, the Greens and Singletons in Glasgow – as well as King's Caledonian Associated Cinemas, and ABC, founded by 'The Chief', John Maxwell. All these – and the Odeon empire from down south. Scotland also had its great and peculiar cathedrals of the movies. Green's Playhouse in Glasgow – the biggest in Europe, the wild Spanish fortress of the Toledo, Muirend, the Viking at Largs, the exotic Windsor at Carluke and the Radio at Kilbirnie. At night cinemas like the Paramount in Glasgow's Renfield Street took on a grand neon splendour.

Managers, projectionists, usherettes, cashiers and chocolate boys might make up a small army in the cities, but in small towns and villages, men and women often ran the show as a family affair or almost single-handed.

The Pavilion in Forfar, known as the Gaff, was owned by the Scott family – Mrs Scott in black silk out front, daughter Jennie acting as usherette, and son Jimmy, in evening dress, patrolling the aisles.

JEAN DUNDAS

In the early years 'tickets' were to be recycled:

The girl in the cash box had in front of her upright rods, on which were entrance discs of different shapes: square, round, and triangular with a hole in the centre. These were handed to the patrons like today's tickets. The shape of disc was in accordance with the part of cinema they were going to. On entering the hall itself the discs were handed to the usherette who threaded these onto a cord round her waist.

BILLIE WILSON

Along with the job came a uniform to be kept neat and smart.

When I left school at 14 in the early 1930s, I got a job in the New Victoria, Edinburgh. There were always big long queues there, going right round St Patrick Square. What I had to do was hang this tray round my shoulders – on it was a small glass ice-cream dish with an artificial ice-cream in it, a cup and saucer, and a tumbler with straws. I walked round the theatre while the films were showing and when I got a customer I had to go upstairs to the cafeteria, put a scoop of ice-cream in a glass dish and then go back with it. No ice-lollies, or choc-ices or tubs in those days. At the back of the stalls there were some private tables to seat about four and for these customers I usually served pots of tea.

MATHILDA ROBERTS

Those who worked in these palaces of pleasure had plenty to deal with.

During a film one evening, Dad became aware of a red trickle flowing through the bottom of the manager's door, and on going to find out what was causing it, he met an usherette and they realised that a man had fallen over in the stalls and was lying – and by this time moaning – on the floor. There had been a sound of broken glass. Dad was trying to get the man on his feet to take him to the office. A phone call was made and soon medical help arrived. By this time the

78

EDINBURGH'S NEW VICTORIA STAFF DECKED OUT FOR THE PREMIERE OF THE JESSIE MATTHEWS TRIUMPH, 'EVERGREEN'. MATHILDA ROBERTS IS SECOND FROM THE RIGHT, FIRST ROW.
(MATHILDA ROBERTS)

80

man was crying. Trying to comfort him, thinking he was in pain, they made out they hoped it was blood that was staining the office floor and not his bottle of whisky.

BILLIE WILSON

THE PROJECTION ROOM AT LA SCALA, DUNOON. (SCOTTISH FILM AND TELEVISION ARCHIVE AT SCOTTISH SCREEN)

Many managers started at the bottom and spent a lifetime on the circuit. Youngsters needed to be watched, however.

After being the spool boy for a while, I got to be a sort of apprentice. The first job they gave me to do was to change the canopy. The first occasion I did it, the manager wasn't happy with me – he had me up and down and up and down as the spacing was all incorrect, so I decided I wasn't going to get a row the next time. I got a piece of graph paper and counted all the letters available and the spaces on the canopy and worked out what I could do the next time.

When it came I went out with the ladders and got on with it. And when I was finished I looked at it and thought: 'Well, he can't complain about the spacing.' I went and got him, and the manager came out, looked at it, and he just shuddered and went sort of apoplectic. He shouted at me, 'Oh for goodness sake, get it down, get it down', and marched back into the cinema.

I looked at it. All the spacing was absolutely perfect. So I read what I had put up:

GEORGE WASHINGTON SLEPT HERE
WITH ANN SHERIDAN

DICK HOLYOAK

City life was only part of the picture. The Orkney Rural Cinema Scheme provided shows for 27 halls throughout the islands.

Despite the operators having to travel many miles by road and sea in all weathers, very few shows were lost as a result. Breakdowns were also few and far between, despite the equipment being loaded and unloaded so many times. At Calf Sound alone, the boxes were loaded into a car, out of the car, down the beach, into a cockleshell of a boat, transferred at sea to a motorboat, then out to the North Isles steamer where they were hauled on board with ropes thrown down from the deck.

At Stronsay my lodgings were with the Stouts, the bakers in the village. No shortage of food here, everything straight from the bakehoose. The hall was quite a way out of the village and again a hired car came for me in time to get things set up and tried out before the public arrived. I seem to remember there was a rather bad echo in the hall, which didn't help the soundtrack of the film. Usually there was an average audience of 96.

In 1953/54 we had 47,732 paying customers and they paid £3,912 and nine pence. The most popular stars were Gregory Peck and Jack Hawkins, Glynis Johns and Jane Wyman. Still, you can't please all of the people all of the time. We had a questionnaire form returned with the complaint: 'We know there are pictures made which are not worth showing, but why send them all to North Ronaldsay?'

IAN CAMERON

From the age of five, I was making a valuable contribution to the entertainment world of the 1950s, albeit as a rewind boy and (eventually) splicing assistant. My dad showed films in the village hall in Craighouse, Jura, on alternate Saturdays at 8.15 pm. There was no mains electricity on the island (there was a native population of about 100) and the shows were made possible by a temperamental generator which ran on tractor vaporising oil. My greatest delight

was when Laurel and Hardy were on the programme. Fortunately my dad and the rest of the audience liked them too, so they became regular attractions.

WILLIE McINTYRE

The show had to go on, whatever the price.

During the War there was a shortage of prints too. Films would get shoved around the country. When I was at the Rialto at Cathcart we were due to show Cecil B De Mille's epic 'The Sign Of The Cross' and on the Monday it hadn't arrived. The renter eventually told us it was coming up from down south and would be at Glasgow Central about 12.30 pm. So I was despatched with string and paper to collect it. The train was late – it steamed in at 1.30 pm. The film was an epic with 16 reels – there was no way I could take 16 reels on the tram. So I took a taxi, it cost half a crown, and when I arrived at the cinema the manager was standing at the door holding back the queue. 'Get up those stairs and get it on.' Once it was on the machine and running I went down to the manager's office and asked for the money for the taxi – 'Oh no laddie, you got the money for the tram. If you want to take a taxi you'll have to pay for it yourself.'

DICK HOLYOAK

At a lesser hall in Dumfriesshire in the '40s, things were decidedly fraught:

When I became a projectionist I got 12/6 a week for four nights and a matinée. I was able to watch the films, but the main problem was the frequent breakages – film piling up on the floor, when the whole audience seemed to erupt in a frenzy – and the boss was climbing up the ladder to the box to give us hell. The projection box hung from the ceiling and the ladder was the only way to get in. The light provided by the carbon arcs was a naked flame of intense heat, and the film was highly inflammable. Health and Safety wouldn't have let us operate now.

JOHN MURRAY

Saved by the cinema …

*During the War my brother Francis was one of the projectionists at the
Baths Hall Cinema. At the time he had just returned from his internment on the
Isle of Man. One Sunday afternoon he and his friends were out for a daunder, and
Francis decided to climb the high pole which carried the electricity supply up Golf
Hill. Off he went, hand over hand, but when he reached the top he inadvertently
swung over and caught the high-tension cable. 11,000 volts shot through his body,
and he fell to the ground flat on his back. At first they said he was dead.*

*I was in a state of shock myself on seeing my brother lying there and don't
remember much, but with the help of a passer-by, Francis regained consciousness,
was taken to Dumfries and eventually returned home to convalesce. When visited
by a friend and asked how he was getting on, he replied, 'I'm OK but my … is
burning', as there was a massive burn on his backside at the point where his hip
pocket, containing the cinema keys, made contact with his flesh.*

EMILIO DICERBO

85

In Glasgow there was more time for pranks …

*It wasn't just film prints that were in short supply in those days.
Everything was short. Food, cigarettes, whisky, you name it. But I never
thought coke would be short. By this time I was in the Coliseum in Eglinton
Street and it was heated by four coke boilers. On this Monday morning we didn't
have enough, and the coke wasn't going to come till the afternoon. There was this
huge building, it had been empty since Saturday, and believe you me in the middle
of winter it was freezing. So when I was going for my lunch there was this small
queue of people waiting for the doors to open. So I got out these cut-outs and put
them outside the front door – icebergs, polar bears and guys in canoes, and a notice*

which said, 'Please come inside, it is cooler here'. Ah dear, the manager was
not very keen when he came back from lunch.

DICK HOLYOAK

THE PARAMOUNT [NOW THE
ODEON], GLASGOW.
(SCOTTISH FILM AND
TELEVISION ARCHIVE
AT SCOTTISH SCREEN)

The news magazine of the industry was the Kine Weekly and we all read
the escapades of 'The Chief': the ongoing story of the projection room staff of a
fictitious super-duper cinema where the chief was higher than God. The people who
staffed cinemas were, in many ways, a breed apart and very dedicated – somehow
touched by the magic of the environment in which they worked. Hours were long; 55
hours a week being common, and pay was poor. On the other hand cinemas were
generally well-staffed, and a hall of 1200 seats I managed in the 1950s had a staff of
20. With the cinema packed to capacity most nights they were all kept
busy and enjoyed what they were doing.

G B MILLAR

Fragrant memories of wartime Glasgow:

When I was trainee manager at the Plaza in Govan, we were going
to show the Greer Garson movie 'Mrs Miniver'. There was a firm who made air
spray for cinemas and they were tying it in with this movie. They had decided that
as Mrs Miniver was given a rose named after her by the station-master in the film,
their new spray would be christened the 'Mrs Miniver Rose'. They had been
demonstrating it in the office one evening when unexpectedly the district manager
walked in, a rather elderly gentleman, and he sniffed the atmosphere, looked
at me and said: 'Good God, this place smells like a brothel.'

DICK HOLYOAK

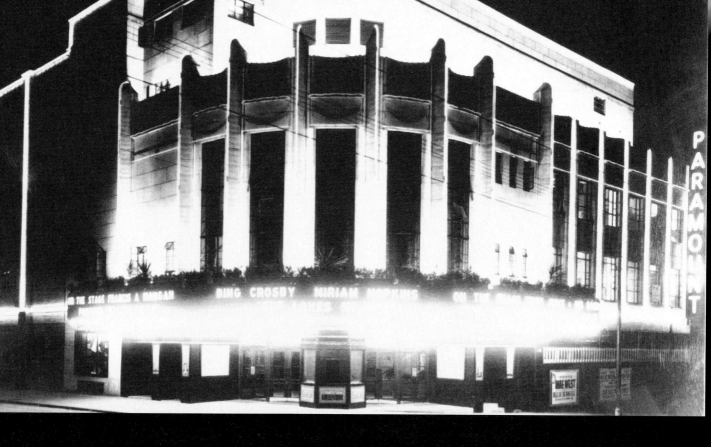

HOLLYWOOD, CALIFORNIA

Dear Friend:

Your letters and interest in me are greatly appreciated. It would be a pleasure to answer personally, if time would permit me doing so.

Thank you so much for writing to me.

Yours sincerely,
HEDY LAMAR

PHOTOGRAPHS

5x7 in. size . . . . . $ .10
8x10 in. size 25

G. Anderson
28 Riverford Rd.
Pollokshaws, Glasgow,
Scotlands. 3

YOU WERE NEVER LOVELIER:
THE STARS

In Glasgow in 1938, one young Scotsman stole a photograph from a cinema. When he appeared in court the sheriff looked at the details of the crime and asked, 'Who is Greta Garbo?' It made news worldwide – there was one person on the planet who had not heard of the world's most famous star. When Mary Pickford and Douglas Fairbanks visited Europe on their honeymoon in 1920, crowds in the street were likened to a revolution. Laurel and Hardy called in at Edinburgh's Playhouse in 1932 and mounted police had to control the masses. When Jeanette MacDonald sought out her Scottish ancestry in Balfron in 1946, a local remarked, 'She jist spoke awa' like an ordinary person'.

In the great days of cinema-going, there was little thought for the expertise of the directors and writers, or the skills of the cinematographer or designer – they were only priests and hand-maidens to the leading players. Their very names were romantic and strange: Dolores Del Rio, Ramon Novarro, Dorothy Lamour, Rock Hudson, Lauren Bacall. Even those with everyday names – Elizabeth Taylor, Joan Crawford, William Holden – were very different from the boys and girls next door. The stars remain an enigma, like their counterparts in the night sky, glittering mysteriously from afar.

We all have our favourites – who knows why? A Falkirk housewife remembers the charms of Alan Ladd, her blond husband at her side. A brunette little girl from Fife dreams of Hedy Lamarr. Many many wartime teenage girls idolise the wholesome charms of Deanna Durbin – Odeons throughout the country gave their public 'Seven Happy Days' with Deanna.

HEDY LAMARR, THE WORLD'S MOST BEAUTIFUL WOMAN, REPLIES TO A GLASGOW FAN. OR DOES SHE? NOTE THE SPELLING ON THE CARD. (SCOTTISH LIFE ARCHIVE)

One middle-aged woman is enthusiastic over Stewart Granger, dismissive of Clark Gable. Merle Oberon's doll-like face enchants one customer, bores another. Why was Audie Murphy so popular? Who swooned over Tab Hunter? And then there was Jeanette MacDonald, not one for little boys or sophisticates, but beloved it seems by everyone else in Scotland.

Some Scots like witty comic players …

THE VIOLET-EYED BEAUTY OF HOLLYWOOD'S LAST REAL STAR, A DOZEN YEARS INTO A GREAT CAREER, IN 1954.

I was called after Irene Dunne. She was my father's favourite film star. My mother's favourite was Melvyn Douglas – my brother is Melvyn.

IRENE MAXWELL

Others liked dark and brooding ones …

I only belonged to one fanclub – James Mason's. He was always my great favourite.

MOLLY BUCHANAN

Or cheerful action heroes …

Audie Murphy – I wanted to marry him.

ANNETTE SHORT

"THE LAST TIME I SAW PARIS" …
"it was Spring and I was in love … with a stranger!"

To my young eyes, the most beautiful Hollywood star was Hedy Lamarr, who seemed too beautiful to be real. But then Hollywood stars weren't real people, which is why folk paid money to see their films. I remember thinking Howard Keel was incredibly good-looking. Even though Mum and I went to see 'Calamity Jane' for a record nine times, I still couldn't figure out what he saw in Doris.

ISLA HELM

'WILL YOU REMEMBER?'
WENT THE SONG IN 1937.
SIX DECADES LATER SCOTS
HAVE NOT FORGOTTEN THE
SINGING SWEETHEARTS.
(TOM MARTIN)

I preferred Westerns, comedies, cartoons – until around 1936 when I saw 'Rose Marie' and fell in love with Jeanette MacDonald. I never missed any of her films, seeing some of them twice in one week.

WILLIAM COOPER

My first hero was Gene Autry, but then I graduated to Errol Flynn, and I think I saw every film made by Abbot and Costello – I can't stand them now! I didn't have a female favourite until adolescence and then my heart throbbed for Virginia Mayo.

F D THORNE

I loved James Cagney – the way he knitted his eyebrows and stuck his chin out.

WALTER WATT

My first heart-throb was Frank Lawton – that was in the early '30s or even before. Greta Garbo was in her prime then, but apart from 'Anna Karenina' I can't recall another film of hers.I didn't care for her anyway.

ELIZABETH HUNTER

Frank Lawton was 'David Copperfield'; Freddie Bartholemew grown-up ...

The one I loved from afar was Franchot Tone. Does anyone apart from me remember him? He was usually the supporting star who rarely got the girl. To me he was Mr Wonderful.

ZENA EUNSON

91

... He was also Mr Joan Crawford.

*My ma was partial to the Bogart, Cagney and George Raft gangster movies,
but most of all she loved a good weepie. Bette Davis, Joan Crawford and
(guaranteed to bring her hotfoot to the ticket kiosk, one and threepence in hand)
Barbara Stanwyck, in my mammy's opinion 'a rare wee greeter'.*

ROBERT DOUGLAS

'BEAUTIFUL DYNAMITE' WAS
THE PHRASE FRED ASTAIRE
USED FOR CYD CHARISSE,
HIS CO-STAR IN 'THE BAND
WAGON', 1953.

*A reliable way to annoy my mother was to comment on her resemblance
to Barbara Stanwyck – she didn't care to have that pointed out, much preferring
to be compared to Paulette Goddard.*

HELEN McCORRY

*I was a real film fan and wrote to all the stars. As a result I had a very
large collection of autographed photographs. What happened to them? I remember
seeing 'Tonight And Every Night' with a girl friend and we danced and sang all
the way home from the Parade Cinema in Meadowpark Street
as would-be Rita Hayworths.*

MAY DUNN

*I loved the early black and white musicals and admired Eleanor Powell
tremendously. 'Broadway Melody Of 1936' was a classic, and she tap-danced her
way to capture the heart of a young Robert Taylor. I wrote to Eleanor Powell
telling her how much I loved the film. Imagine my delight when a photograph
arrived at our house signed: 'To Ethel, from your dancing friend Eleanor.'
It stayed on my bedroom wall for many years.*

ETHEL VAUDREY

Since I went to tap-dancing when I was little,
I suppose my favourite stars were the
big musical dancers such as Ann Miller
(I always hoped I would have legs as long
as her when I grew up – ah well!),
Cyd Charisse; Ginger and Fred of course.
Many of the routines remain with me –
Marilyn Monroe and Jane Russell
duetting in 'Gentlemen Prefer Blondes';
the Gene Kelly umbrella dance routine
in 'Singin' In The Rain'; the barn-
raising hoe-down in 'Seven Brides For
Seven Brothers'. All magic moments.

ISLA HELM

When I heard Jeff Chandler was dying
it upset me a lot as I kept his photo on my wall.

HAZEL GALLOWAY

My first boyhood hero was one who righted wrongs in the Wild West – he was a
gunslinger who went by the name of Johnny Mack Brown. Who? And as far as we
were concerned the lovely Doris Day could do no wrong. Whipcrackaway!

ANGUS BRUCE

My husband's favourite was Ava Gardner, and I remember going to see 'Bhowani Junction' with him. He had been in India and Burma during the War, and I thought that was the attraction, but no, it was Ava.

MABEL CUNNINGHAM

When we were older and saw the Frank Sinatra movies, we loved them. We awaited all his records with great anticipation. In 'It Happened In Brooklyn', Frank stands on the Brooklyn Bridge and sings a lovely song about it. When I went to New York in 1958, my brother made me promise to find the bridge, stand where Frank had stood and sing the song. I promised, but my friend and I got lost in the subway and we never found Brooklyn.

MOLLY BUCHANAN

Movies could be educational, though matinée idols contributed to the learning process.

Were you to ask me 'Who built the Panama Canal?'
Quick as a flash – Tyrone Power!

VALERIE SMITH

Tyrone Power was the heartbreaker of the 1930s and every girl's dream boy. My friends and I saw 'Alexander's Ragtime Band' three times. Years later, seeing him from the front row of the stalls of the Kings Theatre, I was not disappointed. He had retained his figure and good looks. How could one forget his features, sleek black hair, eyebrows, thick eyelashes and deep brown eyes.

LUCINDA ALLAN

The world of Hollywood could even intrude on a quiet Borders countryside in the 1930s, in a hotel once frequented by Hogg and Scott. Appropriately enough the star in question was one of the great romantics.

My hero was Ronald Colman; his best film 'The Prisoner Of Zenda'.
One particular time a lady visitor to Tibbie Shiels Inn, where I lived, saw a big picture I'd cut from a magazine hanging in the wee still room. She asked who his admirer was, and I told her I thought he was so handsome. (Today he's not my type, but in my teens I thought him super.) Anyhow she smiled and said she could get me a better picture of Ronnie, as she called him, a signed one. She was Ronald Colman's sister, and she and her husband were staying at the Inn for the loch fishing. She was as good as her word. In a few weeks a big beautiful signed photograph arrived in the post. I was thrilled. Alas, as I grew older I met and married someone I thought much better, and not in the least like Ronnie. Such is the fancy of youth.

ISABELLE SHAW

Stars could also be inspirational, as the poem on the next pages reveals:

RONALD COLMAN — THE VELVET-VOICED HERO OF 'RANDOM HARVEST', 'ZENDA' AND SHANGRI-LA.

The Grand Circle

One night at Kelty Gothenburg,
Famous for its fleas,
I saw the great Burt Lancaster
In the film 'Trapeze'.
He'd muscles where ah'd never seen
Muscles grow before,
And thon Gina Lollobrigida
Thrilled me to the core.

And so I joined Carnegie Club
For a Gymnast I would be.
Charlie Nesbitt, the instructor
Smiled and said to me;
You want to be a Gymnast, son,
I'm led to understand,
But you'll never be a champion
Until you've done the Grand.

Come over here with me, he said,
And I'll show you a star.
That's John O'Brien away up there
On the horizontal bar.
He'll show you the Grand Circle
So you can set your sights,
And maybe in a year or two
You'll reach those dizzy heights.

But you seem awfy thin tae me
And tho' you're standin' near,
Yiv only tae turn sideways
And you almost disappear.
Whoever sent you to me
Must have been half-canned,
Unless you build some muscle
You'll never do the Grand.

Well, I practised on the Pommel Horse,
I practised on the Rings,
I practised on the Parallel Bars,
But dreamed of higher things,
Did press-ups on the dusty floor
Where I'd danced tae Jimmy Shand,
But I vowed that I would dance no more
Until I'd done the Grand.

The Horizontal Bar at last,
Eight feet above the floor,
Glistening like a Xmas tree,
It made my spirits soar.
For months I practised on the bar
And then my hopes were fanned;
It's now or never, Charlie said.
Tonight, go for the Grand!

96

Remember all I've taught you,
Rub your hands with chalk,
Make sure of a good up start
Then throw to twelve o' clock.
Pause there for a second
Before your downward swing;
But by now I was so nervous
I'd forgotten everything.

My heart was beating like a drum
And tremors shook my knees,
But like a dream, Burt Lancaster
Appeared on his trapeze.
He gave me that big toothy grin
And then held out his hand,
And I jumped up and grasped the bar.
And at last I did the Grand!

JIM DOUGLAS

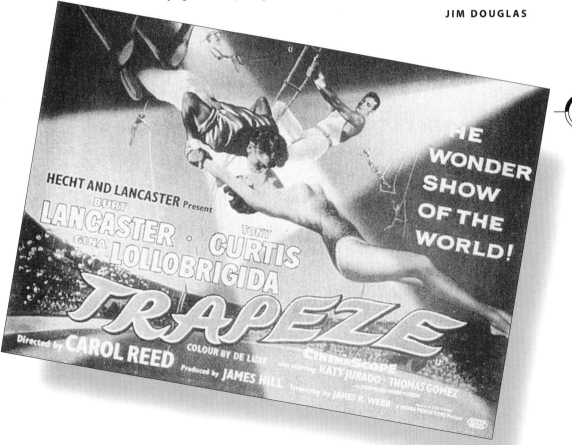

97

Most boys seemed to prefer cowboys, but my hero was
Johnny Weismuller as Tarzan. I thought it was marvellous how he
stayed underwater and fought lions, plus those horrible cannibals who
turned up now and then. It is a pity I was too young to appreciate
Maureen O'Sullivan as his mate, in those skimpy costumes. Now I
understand it was all make-believe but as kids it was real. I used to
hide under my seat when Tarzan struggled with those lions. In fact I
had my own battle-cry when I worked in the shipyards – my workmates
used to laugh at me – it was Tarzan calling the elephants.
My apprentice started using it, so I have left a legend of my hero.

WALTER WATT

Biceps were popular, but so were curls.

Then there were the Shirley Temple films; how I did want to be like her. I
remember 'The Bluebird', happy and sad, and different. I even suffered having my
hair tied up in rags each night to make ringlets like hers – sheer agony, but oh the
joy in the morning to see them emerge from the rags. A friend of my mum's actually
copied the clothes worn by Shirley and made them up for me.

MARGARET LAVERICK

There was a cinema in Stornoway but us youngsters never got there for more
reasons than one. For a start, most parents frowned on the cinema and regarded it
as Devil's work; secondly, cars and buses were few and far between, and thirdly,
money was scarce and wouldn't have stretched to a night out at the flicks. The things
that kept my interest alive were Picture Show *and* Picturegoer, *and the*
glamorous postcard-size pictures available in Woolworths. My number one star was
Alan Ladd. My sister was working in town and kept me supplied.

G C

I went to the pictures at least twice a week. On occasion I went twice a day. I was not unusual in this respect. The effect? At times, perhaps, we didn't know if we were ourselves or gag-happy Hopes, tight-lipped Ladds or fencing Flynns. We males must have bored the pants off (which come to think of it was our intention) our females with tenth-rate impersonations of Danny Kaye and Donald O'Connor. But in turn we paid the price of their pallid presentations of Veronica Lake and Joan Crawford.

JIM BRUNTON

Our young minds idolised Deanna Durbin, Judy Garland, Bette Davis, Joan Crawford and all the other beauties of that time. Betty Grable, Claudette Colbert and Carole Lombard took us into a world of glamour and colour. It was only as we reached 16 or 17 that we noticed Robert Taylor, Gregory Peck and Clark Gable – who all seemed that bit older than us – but they did enliven our romantic awareness.

ELSPETH BEATON

I went to anything and everything. At a ridiculously unsuitable age I saw Joan Crawford in 'The Bride Wore Red' – such decadence! These glamorous women were like family to me: Joan Bennett, Constance Bennett, Carole Lombard, Katharine Hepburn, Myrna Loy – so elegant, but funny – and Claudette Colbert who wore the most amazing hats! I also recall with affection Eve Arden; she could deliver the most hilarious lines with a dead-pan face and an offhand manner. Deanna Durbin – I'm not sure she could act, but she could sing. I still play

tapes of her songs and I still wish I could sing like her. And all those wonderful Astaire and Rogers films. After an evening in their company I would try to reproduce Ginger's steps in front of my mirror, but alas it needed Fred Astaire.

ZENA EUNSON

We copied the stars. I liked to dress up and pretend to be Ginger Rogers, dancing cheek-to-cheek. Deanna Durbin made a huge impression – my mother knitted me a hat from a magazine pattern which was supposed to be like one Deanna wore in 'One Hundred Men And A Girl'. We also sported bubble-cut hairstyles after Ingrid Bergman in 'For Whom The Bell Tolls'. I also had a Robin Hood (Errol Flynn) hat with a feather!

HELEN McNIE

The most rewarding bonus from all this cinema-going was the glamour of the actresses and our efforts to emulate them. We searched high and low for the make-up of the stars, Max Factor. Shampoo was advertised as used for shining results by Rita Hayworth, Betty Grable and so on. We sewed accessories to brighten our tired wardrobes, we polished our shoes and straightened our stockings, even if it had all been borrowed from the rest of our family. Our young men had no complaints. And if Joan Crawford could sport a fur coat with a bunch of violets on the lapel, we had a bunch of violets too, discovered in Granny's workbox.

VALERIE SMITH

On a very few occasions, contact with the stars went one step further:

EVERY SCHOOLGIRL'S IDOL – THE COLORATURA CHARMS OF DEANNA DURBIN, IN HAPPY RETIREMENT SINCE 1949. (LUCINDA ALLAN)

100

I once met James Stewart on Princes Street in Edinburgh. He was in the American Air Force then, and we bumped into one another. He put his hands on my shoulders and said 'I'm so sorry'.

CATHERINE JARVIS

After the War, Grace Godley and her husband went off to America to be a cook/housekeeper and butler, and found themselves in Hollywood. As a girl, Grace was not 'much of a one for film stars' ...

In front of us in the plane was James Mason, so that was the first glimpse of a film star. In Los Angeles the friends we made, British couples, all worked for well-known names such as Darryl Zanuck, the producer, Jean Simmons and Stewart Granger. We went to work for Glenn Ford. He would take us to the studio and show us previews of his films. Our next-door neighbour then was Rita Hayworth. Then we went to Debbie Reynolds. It was a very busy and very happy household. Debbie was a very kind person and treated us as family.

GRACE GODLEY

In 1956 I entered a competition run by The Sunday Dispatch *to meet the Hollywood legend Miss Joan Crawford while she was in Britain filming 'The Story Of Esther Costello' at Shepperton Studios. The competition involved dreaming-up a question you would put to Joan and her suggested reply. I was the Scottish winner with the following entry ...*

To Joan: 'Can you tell me Joan, which of your leading men kissed you the best?'

Joan's reply: 'I would, if I could, but I can't.'

On 27th September 1956, after making the only air flight of my life, I had a lovely day meeting Joan and the other stars of the film, Rossano Brazzi and Heather Sears. On the next set were Jack Hawkins and Arlene Dahl and also working there that day was Tyrone Power.

The studio had arranged for a closed set that day, and Joan toured the set showing us the different rooms and my first impression was how small and dainty she was, the way she walked and the gorgeous gowns she wore. Miss Crawford was delightful to everyone, giving each of the six regional winners a red rose. I still have that red rose (pressed of course and only a stem remains) as a memento of a day I will never forget.

I kept regular contact with Joan and her last letter arrived a week after she died in 1977. As usual her letter finished with the words 'Bless you Violet'.

VIOLET CRUICKSHANK

We came out of the cinema one night and the evening newspaper billboard had 'The King is dead'. This was the news of the death of Clark Gable.

MARGARET BEATON

MISS JOAN CRAWFORD MEETS HER FANS IN THE FOURTH DECADE OF HER STARDOM. VIOLET CRUIKSHANK IS SECOND FROM THE RIGHT. (VIOLET CRUIKSHANK)

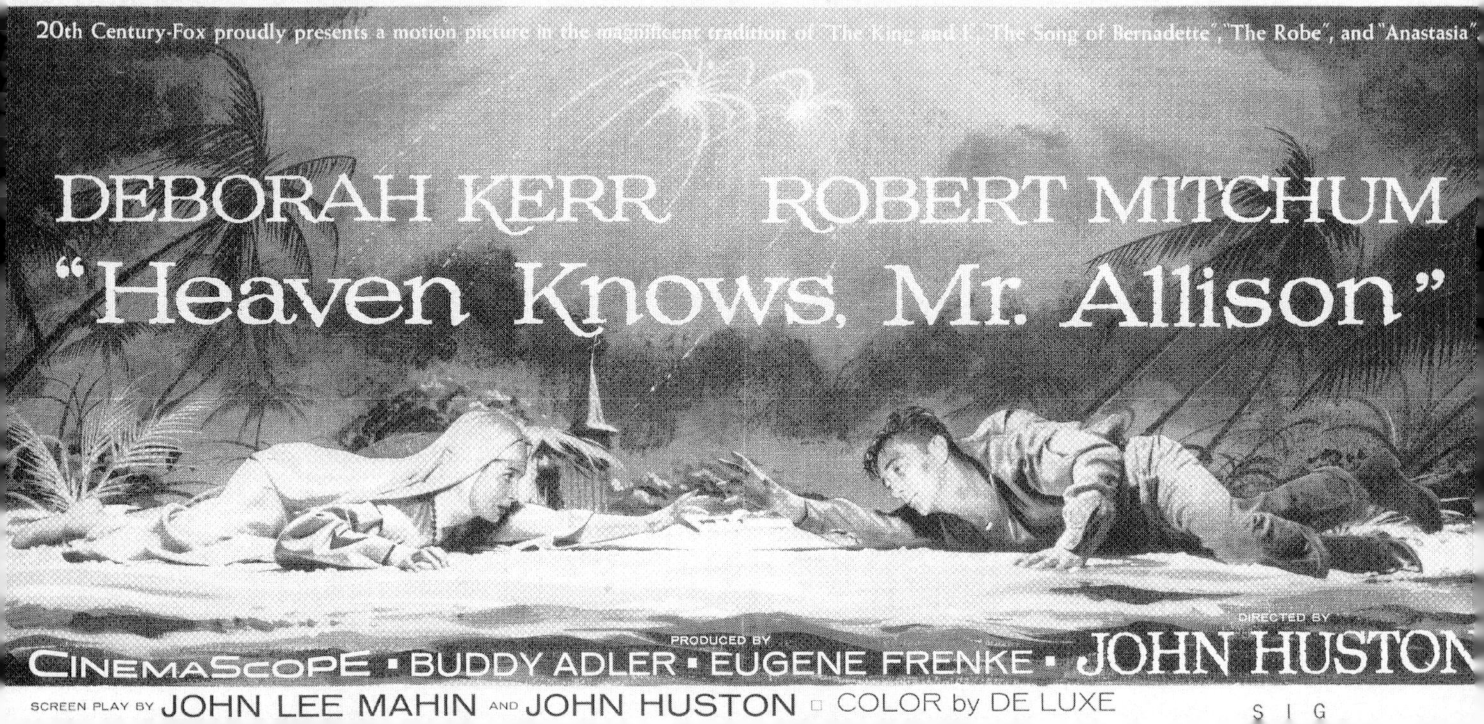
20th Century-Fox proudly presents a motion picture in the magnificent tradition of "The King and I", "The Song of Bernadette", "The Robe", and "Anastasia"
DEBORAH KERR ROBERT MITCHUM
"Heaven Knows, Mr. Allison"
PRODUCED BY
DIRECTED BY
CINEMASCOPE • BUDDY ADLER • EUGENE FRENKE • JOHN HUSTON
SCREEN PLAY BY JOHN LEE MAHIN AND JOHN HUSTON □ COLOR by DE LUXE
S I G

HIGH, WIDE AND HANDSOME:
BIG SCREEN IN THE 1950s

The arrival of television in America frightened the big studios, as audiences stayed at home to watch quiz shows. In Britain television grabbed its chance with the Coronation in 1953, where the ceremonies arrived in darkened living-rooms throughout the land. If the cinema was to compete, it had to offer something that no living-room could contain. The studios looked once more to invention and gimmickry to tempt people back to the stalls.

For a few moments the future seemed to lie with Cinerama, a huge widescreen system ideal for spectacular travelogues, less so for drama – then it was 3D, Warner's Natural Vision. The audience wore green and red specs and ducked anything the stereoscopic camera saw fit to throw at them – arrows, lions, high-kicking legs. But it was CinemaScope which proved the most durable innovation. From 1953 films would be wider – a letterbox shape – and colour would be obligatory. The intimate dramas of the past were out of place on a screen which could not handle close-ups or even romantic clinches. What CinemaScope and its rivals could handle superbly well was *spectacle*. Even the stars of the 1950s were brasher – beefcake joined cheesecake to fill the landscapes required for the new ratio. Historical epics, glossy dramas in exotic locales and big musicals were the norm, and were the big earners.

SCOTLAND'S GIFT TO HOLLYWOOD, DEBORAH KERR, GETS TO KNOW ONE OF HER FAVOURITE LEADING MEN ON A SOUTH PACIFIC ISLAND, 1957.

The biggest surprise I remember was the introduction of 3D. We were issued with cardboard glasses of universal size – pity if your head wasn't average! One lens was green and the other red. The film was 'House Of Wax'. The whole audience screamed when the ball hurled towards us.

MARGARET BEATON

105

*Even the adverts were in 3D – showers of cigarettes seemed
to come out over the audience!*

HELEN McNIE

*Half-way through the movie there was a heavy dunt followed by a howl, as some
man a few seats in front ducked too low to avoid a knife thrown by Vincent Price
and hit his forehead off the back of the head of the patron in front.*

ROBERT DOUGLAS

*CinemaScope arrived courtesy of 20th Century-Fox. I was a manager
in Dundee then and my cinema The Broadway was one of the first to be
equipped for this new medium. With it came magnetic soundtracks and
stereophonic sound in cinemas able to afford the new equipment.*

G B MILLAR

Screens widened first of all for 'The Robe'.

*At last the lights went down and the curtains opened to what
appeared to be just a normal size screen and the then-familiar 20th Century-Fox
logo and music came on. Sammy and I looked at each other – dead disappointed.
'Disnae look very big tae me,' said Sammy. 'Naw,' said I. Then the screen went
blank and the curtains opened until there in front of us was a curved screen, not
only taller but three times wider than normal. A voice said 'Ladies and Gentlemen,
this is CinemaScope!' and on again came the logo, but this time filling the giant
screen and accompanied – in stereophonic sound – by a revamped version of the
signature tune, which ended on a rising crescendo only used for CinemaScope. The
hair on the back of our necks tingled, there was a collective 'ooh!' from the audience.
Sammy and I looked at each other – crickey jings!*

ROBERT DOUGLAS

The Biblical epic had been absent from the screen since the Silents, when Cecil B DeMille ransacked the Book of Judges for 'Samson And Delilah' in 1950. It was soon to become staple fare on the big, improved screen.

The really big pictures, of course, with the original casts of thousands, were the likes of 'The Robe', 'Demetrius And The Gladiators' (the follow-up), 'Ben-Hur' and 'The Ten Commandments'. The whole audience seemed to emerge from that in hushed reverence. This was of course in the days when the Kirk was not to be mocked, even if you didn't go yourself!

ISLA HELM

Called up for National Service, I remember 'Kiss Me Kate' with Howard Keel and Kathryn Grayson shown in a billet hut, but using the very latest in stereophonic sound equipment. The RAF always bought the latest and best equipment, but it was meant to be used in an Odeon. In such a small area the effect was out of this world – everything was larger than life. A great experience.

FREDDIE MARTIN

And there was the chance to see irsels as ithers see us ...

From the Scottish viewpoint, pictures like 'Whisky Galore!' and 'Geordie' obviously went down very well. There was much laughter at the sight of the islanders stashing the bottles of whisky from the wrecked ship, when for most of the men in the audiences anyway, their only other extravagances besides going to the pictures, were cigarettes and a guid bucket at the weekend. 'Geordie' on the other hand appealed shamelessly to Scottish patriotism, and Scottish chests swelled with pride as the eponymous Geordie marched defiantly alone, wearing his dead father's kilt, in the Olympic parade. Even 'Brigadoon' was accepted unquestionably as a braw picture, although the accents were a bit suspect to say the least!

ISLA HELM

The cinema also had one major rival emerging in the 1950s – teenagers found a culture of their own in the world of rock n' roll and pop music. Elvis might be a movie star, but he was equally popular off-screen via the juke-box, transistor and portable record-player. A 74-minute second feature from Columbia with guest acts electrified the world. Audrey Hepburn, Todd-AO and a cast of thousands were all very well, but a very small film caught the mood of the world. It was a flavour of things to come.

JUNE ALLYSON, LAUREN BACALL AND ARLENE DAHL LINE UP IN CARDBOARD IN THE FOYER OF THE BROADWAY, DUNDEE. (G B MILLAR)

The Empire cinema in Clydebank made the national newspapers one time and I missed it because I had gone with some of my pals to Rothesey for the weekend. Rock and roll was the big thing and the film going the rounds was 'Rock Around The Clock' with Bill Haley and the Comets. Apparently it caused a riot, with Bankie teenagers jumping out of their seats and jiving in the aisles. It was reported that the police had to be called to restore order and everyone was evacuated from the cinema. I heard that all sorts of damage was caused and the hall was almost wrecked.

CHRISTINA BYRNE

The same fever of the times hit Fraserburgh …

I remember there were St John's Ambulance people standing at the back, to be on hand if anyone suffered from hysteria. When the picture finished, the local teddy boys and girls with circular skirts started doing the rock and roll in the aisles.

Then they continued outside and the cinema-goers formed a big circle round them to watch. The police moved everyone along, but they started again in the next street.

ISOBEL GREGORY

… and was repeated in the capital:

My mum and dad and I went to the Grand in the late 50s to see 'Rock Around The Clock'. The whole picture house was jumping with the music, but a group of youths behind us were particularly noisy and my mum turned round to give them a telling off – only to discover it was my brother and his friends who were making the racket!

ELAINE BELL

There was still a place for the melodies of yesteryear of course, but sometimes Mario Lanza could outstay his welcome.

We lived in a flat next to the Playhouse in Aberdeen. One hot summer we opened our window as it was so stuffy, and the projectionist – also feeling the heat – opened not only his window but the door as well. Now, I enjoyed 'The Student Prince' when I first saw it, but listening to the soundtrack for nearly three days was a bit much – I think I knew every word of that film.

HUGH McLEOD

There were still those who thought the cinema rather common.

My mother was not a great fan of the cinema. She considered it rather unladylike, and as being ladylike was her raison d'etre, my brother and I did not see many films in the 1950s. My mother did however relent about 1958. My grandfather,

*who was living in a nursing home at the time, had
a fall. Under the circumstances we were rather in
the way, so despite my mother's opinion that (a)
you were likely to catch something if you went to
the cinema and (b) you should definitely not lean
your head back because the seats were likely to be
heaving with fleas, she actually gave my brother
some money and said, 'Why don't you two go to
the cinema?' It was a situation that had never happened before.
I vividly remember that the film we went to see was 'The Inn Of The Sixth
Happiness' with Ingrid Bergman – I wept buckets.*

EDITH PHILIP

Memories of a holiday in Mallaig in the 1950s, when 'Sayonara' brought the
Orient to the west coast.

*The village hall was well filled, and I found myself sitting next to the
crew of one of the local fishing boats, who had obviously just come ashore and were
still in their sea-going garb, which included vast thigh-length sea boots and an all-
pervading aroma of fish. The film began but something was severely wrong with the
local technology – the soundtrack was a muffled, unintelligible mumble. However,
the fishermen supplied any and all sound effects required. In addition, they had huge
bags of sweeties which were passed round the audience with loud encouragement to
everyone to help themselves. Curiously, I've never, in all the intervening years,
managed to see this film on an occasion when its soundtrack was in working order,
so I never have been able to figure out what it was about.*

WYNNE HARLEY

Easily solved. It was about a Japanese actress who played a man, a Japanese actor (played by a Mexican star) who played a woman, two American GIs and a double suicide.

Back in 1955, aged 13, I tripped along alone to Green's Playhouse in Wishaw to catch 'The Sea Chase', an ocean-going saga set in World War II which had John Wayne playing a German merchant ship captain. All the talk in the school-yard was of the incident in which a young sailor has his leg bitten off by a shark. A shark-biting episode was something quite new to us and was therefore something to look forward to with a certain amount of excitement and trepidation. Some way during the film, however, I was approached by an usherette who asked me to run out to the chip shop across the street and get her a bag of same for her tea. I was well-used to running errands for adults and complied without a murmur. But the chip shop was not yet opened and I returned to the cinema to offer my apologies. The usherette was not best pleased and further requested that I run out to the next nearest chip shop, which seemed a long way off. I protested and the lady backed off huffily. Of course, you've guessed it, that annoying little episode caused me to be absent from my seat during the sequence involving the shark.

JOHN McKILLOP

My mother took me to the pictures a lot. Mostly I remember us laughing ourselves silly over the cartoons. My favourite was 'Bugs Bunny' but 'Tweety Pie and Sylvester' came close. 'Will you shoot me now, or will you take me home first?' he said, which still makes me giggle. By and large I was a well-behaved child, but I loved Sylvester's wickedness, his feline equivalent of curling moustaches, and his gleeful greed. I had a '78 of 'I tawt I saw a puddy tat,' which I played so often that my mother sat on it. She said it was an accident, but we knew better.

HELEN McCORRY

LOVE ME OR LEAVE ME:
THE SMALL SCREEN CONQUERS

By the 1960s the whole idea of going to the pictures had lost some of its glamour. Many of the generation who had grown up with the weekly habit were now comfortably at home, listening to a hi-fi, watching television, getting involved in DIY, or going out for a spin in the family car. Teenagers were sticking pop stars on bedroom walls, buying records, and screaming at The Beatles.

The big films were bigger than ever. Most of the studios were in their final years, still bravely operating as dream factories, but their dreams began to seem decidedly anachronistic, and they were wisely moving into television production. Films tended to be events; expensive productions streamlined to appeal to a mass audience. It often worked, but sometimes plans went awry and studio fortunes plummeted. 'Cleopatra' – which premièred in Edinburgh with a young lady taking a milk bath in the foyer – cost so much that even its box office triumph could not save it. Luckily Fox's finances were salvaged by a singing nun in the Austrian Alps. The balance sheet became a major feature in Hollywood, and in the years that followed, MGM, Fox, Paramount, and the rest would lose their distinctive identities and become simply subsidiaries in a world of international companies.

At MGM's Culver City, the studio sold off its props and costumes and demolished its sets. Judy Garland's ruby slippers and Garbo's gowns went under the hammer. The backlot vanished to make way for real estate. No Los Angeles museum recorded Hollywood's past. Old-timers found work in guest spots in television, and Bette Davis and Joan Crawford threw away their glamorous images to play grotesques in horror flicks.

ANTIQUITY'S MOST FAMOUS LOVERS, AS PORTRAYED BY THEIR MODERN COUNTERPARTS IN 1963.

113

Minor players in the studio game would take advantage of relaxed attitudes to censorship and step into a world of exploitation, terror, and sex. Curious audiences would venture out to taste the wares.

Going to the pictures is still an enjoyable experience, but the feeling of occasion has been lost. Families dressed up and met other neighbours and families in the queues. It was a socially significant event in earlier times – not least when you started 'winching' and graduated to the back row with the boyfriend and a box of chocolates. Television made us all islands. We traded the banter and suppressed excitement of the cinema queue for the lazy comfort of the living-room on a cold wet night.

ELLEN CUNNINGHAM

I was in the Odeon, Kirkcaldy, one Saturday afternoon in 1966 watching a cowboy film. During a fight scene the screen suddenly went dark and a still appeared – 'England 4 West Germany 2'. This was greeted by total silence, then there were a few soft groans, then the fight continued as if nothing had happened.

JOHN WYLLIE

There were still attractions which audiences would queue up for, however. The Disneys, old and new, came round again and again. 'Gone With The Wind', carefully protected from television exposure, still had life left in it. There was 'Mary Poppins' and 'My Fair Lady'. And there was the film which became for a while the most popular of all time. It became the film that people would see again and again throughout the 1960s.

The one thing I remember about the Odeon was going to 'The Sound Of Music'. Round the walls of the Odeon, in niches, were statues (they are still there), and I thought they were all Julie Andrews, put there especially for the film.

ELAINE GREIG

The Playhouse and the Pavilion were the venues
in Gala. Saturday pm let loose with my aunties,
the Finlay sisters, some say the best-dressed in the
town. It was a getting-dolled-up sort of occasion.
Names that spring to mind: Rossano Brazzi,
Rock Hudson of course and a lot of melodrama
and the odd submarine. I ate my first
'Amazin Raisin' bar at the pictures. 'Paynes
Poppets' – need I say more! Coming back out
into daylight made it seem really edgy, even at age
six. It all continued back home after an open bag of chips from Vladas;
my auntie at the piano – 'Three Coins In The Fountain' was a regular number!

SUSAN LAMB

The films at Newton Stewart picture house finished at around 10.10 pm.
This was fine if you lived in Newton Stewart and could walk home. If you lived in
one of the outlying villages, however, you had to catch the bus at 10 pm. This meant
that at ten to ten without fail, half of the audience stood up and left. There must be
an entire generation of people in Whithorn, Wigtown, Garlieston and
Port William who never saw the end of anything!

ELAINE WYLLIE

Colouring competitions in the **Dumfries Standard** furnished prizes and free trips
to the blockbusters of the time. For 'My Fair Lady' we left school early and arrived
at the Regal as Audrey once more fetched the slippers for Rex, and then saw the
whole film from the beginning again. Even then it seemed to me that Miss Hepburn
was unusually thin, though some memory tells me that the projection was awry, and
that the Panavision image squeezed Eliza into a decorative beanpole. What was

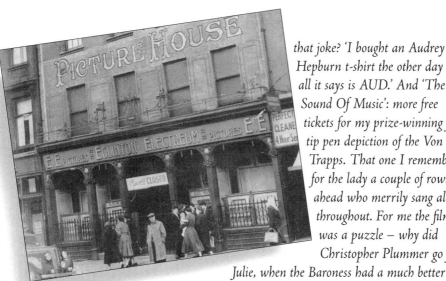

that joke? *'I bought an Audrey Hepburn t-shirt the other day – all it says is AUD.'* And *'The Sound Of Music'*: more free tickets for my prize-winning felt-tip pen depiction of the Von Trapps. That one I remember for the lady a couple of rows ahead who merrily sang along throughout. For me the film was a puzzle – why did Christopher Plummer go for Julie, when the Baroness had a much better wardrobe, and furthermore was allowed to wear make-up?

ANDREW STOBA

A few big pictures for the mums and aunties were not enough to keep the great cavernous picture places open. Throughout Scotland the small town cinemas closed their doors, at least for film-shows. Bingo became a feature for the very participants who had once queued up to see Robert Mitchum and Susan Hayward. Splendid auditoria were decorated with the gaudy paraphernalia of a new popular attraction. Some buildings were converted to shops or stores; the Art Deco lines of the façade a faint reminder of a more lyrical past. Projectors gathered dust in abandoned booths, too heavy to move. Some of the La Scalas and Palaces disappeared altogether, demolished to make way for shopping centres and car parks. In the cities there were desperate attempts to keep the business alive, even if the classy product of the golden days was nowhere to be seen.

Changing times allowed different sorts of spectacles on the screen.

When Sunday opening was approved in the early 1960s, the Church of Scotland expressed concern as to what sorts of film would be shown on the Sabbath. Nuns and children were presumably safe topics, but there were some dodgy epics going the rounds too. And as we see in these Glasgow memories, the cinema-going habit was a difficult one to break. Movies could be educational, but in quite the wrong way.

I go to the pictures with my pal, Betty. We've been going every week for the last 35 years. One time we queued for a film at the Odeon, Renfield Street, but by the time we got to the pay-box there were no seats left. We had seen everything else at the Odeon, so decided to go to the Classic which was further down Renfield Street. The film was advertised as a love story starring a well-known Hollywood actor so we expected to enjoy it. It wasn't long started when we realised that it wasn't the usual love story but was definitely in the category of hard-core porn, which at first I found a bit of giggle. Eventually, however, it got to the stage when I just couldn't watch it.

Unfortunately we were right in the middle of the row and had to squeeze past about ten men to get out. That was when it dawned on us. We were the only women in the cinema. No wonder the cashier had given us an odd look when we bought the tickets.

CHRISTINA BYRNE

The man who had once exhibited Sheridan, Colbert and Garson so proudly now had a different kind of product to promote.

Eventually I was the manager of the Waverley Cinema in Shawlands. And we tried everything to keep the audience coming – we put in CinemaScope, 3D, stereophonic sound. But it was very difficult, and we were failing. Then the

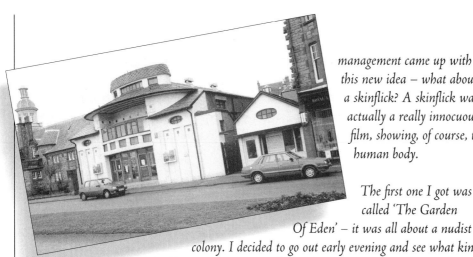

management came up with this new idea – what about a skinflick? A skinflick was actually a really innocuous film, showing, of course, the human body.

The first one I got was called 'The Garden Of Eden' – it was all about a nudist colony. I decided to go out early evening and see what kind of audience the film was attracting and to make sure that none of the under-16s were getting in, which was difficult.

As I was standing, I looked out and here were two old ladies, very regular customers too. And I thought, 'What on earth are they coming to this thing for?' However they marched in, one went to the pay-box and the other came to me.

'Now Mr Holyoak – thet film you showed last week, we did not enjoy. But we're fair looking forward to the one you've got on tonight.' … 'Are you?' … 'Yes, we do like Biblical pictures.' Needless to say, I was not out there to see them out.

DICK HOLYOAK

Cinema-going was not dead, however. The industry responded to changing tastes and times by dividing the great auditoria up, providing smaller screens and more choice. There were still films around to attract the masses, but the cinema was no longer a universal focus. In the 1980s and '90s, new cinemas were built out of town, close to giant superstores, with good parking and junk food on offer, and an eye on the young. In rural districts

118

the old travelling screens have even been revived, bringing cinema to a television generation.

A few of the old cinemas remain: Campbeltown, for example, and Newton Stewart still welcome audiences as they have for most part of a century; still projecting faces on a screen. Other halls, however changed, give glimpses of a past grandeur in a stray detail perhaps – the line of the frontage; the sweep of the balcony; the stars twinkling on the ceiling. They have survived many changes. Eloquent silent faces, chattering Talkies, garish colour treats, panoramic epics and smutty romps. And the films and the personalities linger on, if not always on the big screen, then on television and video, and in that most enduring of cinemas, memory.

On a visit in 1988 I took a run up through Maryhill. Just after passing where the long-gone Seamore had stood, my heart sank – the Blythswood was gone. Stopping the car, we walked over to the rubble-strewn site. Still to be seen were the couple of steps up to the entrance and the black and white tiles of the foyer. Amongst the broken bricks I found two sizeable pieces of white alabaster; all that remained of the mock marble façade. So I took them as my final souvenir of the Blythsie, and they're now placed in a flower bed out the back of our house. Sometimes, sitting out there on a summer's evening, if they catch my eye they can soon transport me back to days of trams, tenements, and going tae the pictures with my mammy.

ROBERT DOUGLAS

Hundreds of people contributed to this book. All remembered with affection the wonders of the big screen. In cinema's great days, audiences from Aberdeen to Wishaw responded to Hollywood's dreams, and wove some of their own. In those darkened cinemas throughout the land Scots were not alone – for a while at least the whole world was dreaming the same dream.

BONNIE SCOTLAND:
ON THE BIG SCREEN

Wha's like us? Mary Pickford in a tammy? Katharine Hepburn as Mary Stuart? Cyd Charisse as Fiona? Richard Todd as Rob Roy? Bill Travers as Geordie? Mel Gibson as the Wallace? All Scots on the screen. Donald Crisp, Jack Buchanan, Deborah Kerr, David Niven and Sean Connery have been up there too, playing shepherds, spies, sophisticates, sluts, but rarely Scots. Ewan McGregor has been both Leith junkie and 'Star Wars' hero. Behind the camera there have been other fine Scottish talents: people who wrote for Garbo; set Charles Laughton adrift from 'The Bounty'; captured 'The Maggie' as well as 'The Sweet Smell Of Success', and painted the yellow brick road. There have even been attempts at a cinema industry, talk of studios, and celebrated exiles returning to revitalise a neglected art form.

A survey of a century of Scotland on the screen can only be a speeded-up reel of hasty clips – a shot of a star here, a bit of scenery there, entire careers summed up in a line. All those fine documentaries have been set aside, and a very personal choice made of who should be spotlighted and who is left on the cutting room floor.

On screen we have never quite thrown off the familiar images derived from Sir Walter Scott or Sir Harry Lauder. Most of these 'Scottish' films came from America, but when we did get the chance to create our own dramas they tended to fall into another stereotype altogether. Dismissing the kailyard we embraced the hard men of a post-industrial country in decline 100 years after music hall Scotchmen fell about on a flickering screen for our amusement; and it took a diminutive Hollywood star to tell Scots a version of their own history, and to stir up pride and excitement.

A FINE FIGURE OF A NATIONAL HERO, COURTESY OF WALT DISNEY– RICHARD TODD AS 'ROB ROY: THE HIGHLAND ROGUE', 1953. (BRITISH FILM INSTITUTE)

121

SILENT SCOTLAND

The early days of cinema ransacked familiar novels, plays and ideas for properties, and found in Scotland an ideal source. No film-goer in the 1900s could have been unaware of a small northern country where the inhabitants were lovesick and noble, honourable and brave, or cheerily peculiar. Throughout the silent days, Scotland could be relied upon for hearty fare, a dash of romance, a dash of action, a flash of scenery, and a tartan trew or two.

From 1898 there were many filmed sketches with a Scottish theme: dancing Highlanders, Gretna Green runaways, Harry Lauder and his imitators in embarrassing situations. But soon there were more ambitious depictions – a French Mary Stuart made her bow in 1908, as did Vitagraph's 'A Chieftain's Revenge' and 'Macbeth'. In 1909 there was another, Italian, 'Macbeth', a 'Lochinvar' and 'The Bride Of Lammermoor'. Florence Turner, the Vitagraph Girl, and Maurice Costello – two of the screen's first stars – were playing in 'Auld Robin Gray' in 1910. Miss Turner was 'The Shepherd Lassie Of Argyle' in 1914. There were new Macbeths and Mary Stuarts almost every year, various Lochinvars, and Annie Lauries. Scotland was everywhere.

Rob Roy made his screen debut in 1911, with John Clyde starring in the first feature to be made in Scotland, and the most ambitious film produced in Britain up to that time. It was filmed on location near Aberfoyle, and in THE QUEEN OF a converted tram depot at Rouken Glen. A great success, there were soon HOLLYWOOD AS 'PRIDE two rival versions. That same year Inverness premièred its very own drama OF THE CLAN' – MARY – 'Mairi, The Romance Of A Highland Maiden', filmed on the coast at PICKFORD IN 1917. North Kessock by local photographer Andrew Paterson. Many Scots film-(BRITISH FILM INSTITUTE) makers of the time captured local events on film – visiting dignitaries, festivities, factory workers – but a dramatic short like 'Mairi' was unusual. A simple love triangle of a smuggler, an exciseman and the eponymous heroine, it had no Scottish trappings.

Scottish films, as opposed to the American version, did have a few further attempts to get off the ground. Rouken Glen at Thornliebank – potentially Scotland's own Hollywood – had to cope with problems of power supply caused by passing trams, but was reborn after World War I with 'The Harp King' – proudly heralded as Scotland's own production. A tale of a harpist and a laird's daughter, it was well-received. The studio's next production 'Football Daft', with location scenes at Ibrox, was also much-liked and seen all over Britain. These were isolated attempts at an industry, however, and most Scots film types were seeking careers not on the outskirts of Glasgow, but in California.

Aberfeldy's Donald Crisp embarked on a long directing and acting career, appearing in 'The Birth Of A Nation'. James Finlayson from Falkirk was the foil to (amongst others) Laurel and Hardy, and Dunoon's Eric Campbell was a memorable heavy to Chaplin. Frank Lloyd was starting his career as actor then director. Reginald Barker, from Bothwell, made the mafia epic 'The Italian' in 1916. Lorna Moon from Strichen found distinction as a scriptwriter, wrote for Garbo, and was close to the De Milles. Frank Lloyd later won Oscars for his directing of such famed productions as 'Cavalcade' and 'Mutiny On The Bounty'.

Many American and British actors were all too keen to wrap the plaid around their shoulders, and Scottish whimsy and the kailyard were weel to the fore. Mary Pickford, the biggest star of all, and sweetheart of all the world whatever language it spoke, was 'The Pride Of The Clan' in 1917 and as Margaret McTavish looked fetching in her tartan tammy. With a big budget and artistic direction by Maurice Tourneur, there was praise for its recreation of a Scots fishing village, and for Pickford's spirited playing. 'The Lilac Sunbonnet' and 'Beside The Bonnie Brier Bush' – infamous titles both

– were filmed; the latter directed by its star, Donald Crisp. There was J M Barrie too of course, even silent. 'The Little Minister' played in various different versions, and 'What Every Woman Knows' followed.

Old plays, old songs and old queens were pulled into service by American and British film-makers alike. Ivor Novello brought his fine profile to 'Bonnie Prince Charlie', Fay Compton brought hers to 'The Loves Of Mary Queen of Scots'. Sophisticate Leatrice Joy, wife of John Gilbert, found herself in Goldwyn's version of 'Bunty Pulls The Strings', directed by Scots exile Reginald Barker. Lillian Gish was 'Annie Laurie' for MGM in a tale which drew on the Massacre of Glencoe. At home an enterprising Englishman saw a future for Robert Burns and Walter Scott on the screen with his 'Immortals Of Bonnie Scotland' – the 'ploughman poet' proved more popular than the 'wizard of the north'. Sir Harry Lauder, who had filmed and abandoned features in dismay before, had a go at some John Buchan in 'Huntingtower'.

SCOTLAND TALKS

With sound, a new element was introduced – the accent. Hollywood was lucky to have a troupe of exile players who could handle it, and J M Barrie's ageing charm was given another outing, this time with words. Donald Crisp, Andy Clyde and Mary Gordon stayed in the shadows while Katharine Hepburn's celebrated Yankee twang tackled Babbie in 'The Little Minister'. Helen Hayes preserved her stage triumph in 'What Every Woman Knows' on celluloid, perhaps not with the Borders lilt, but with Crisp and David Torrence.

It was either Thrums or Pathans for a while. The whole British Empire it seemed was overrun with Scottish Highlanders. Bagpipes resounded courtesy of Fox's Movietone throughout 'The Black Watch', reminding us that it was us Scots (and Victor McLaglen) who saved the North-west frontier. McLaglen's speciality was Oirish, but he did it all again later in 'Wee Willie Winkie', with Shirley Temple no less, and again in 'Gunga Din', where kilts and pipes act as backdrop to the cockney antics of Grant and Fairbanks jnr. 'Will Ye No Come Back Again?' rings out as the regiment marches into a trap. 'The Drum' had a Highland fling danced by our brave lads to bewilder the treacherous locals, and Technicolor tartans. The fondly remembered 'Bonnie Scotland' had Laurel and Hardy, a little of Scotland, and a lot of India, as the hapless pair sought a Scottish inheritance but found the army instead.

There was still a place for the romance of yesteryear however. Katharine Hepburn played the lady straight off the shortbread tin, in tartan as well as black velvet. 'Mary Of Scotland' remains spellbinding for the sheer boldness of its attack. While we may be thankful that Ginger Rogers did not get her wish to be Queen Elizabeth, who would want to have missed Fredric

ROBERT DONAT'S LAIRD MEETS HIS ANCESTOR IN 'THE GHOST GOES WEST', 1935. (EDINBURGH FILM GUILD)

March's Bothwell warming his bare legs by a Holyrood fireplace, or the final scenes at Fotheringay with Mary ascending to her death in a thunderstorm?

Minor British companies did not forget the Scottish factor – old favourites like the Loch Ness monster, the Jacobites, Robert Burns and Harry Lauder were all run out again. But it was the time of Quota Quickies, and only Korda and Gaumont-British could hold a candle to Hollywood imports as audiences and critics showed.

At Elstree, a different class of Scottish adventure was in hand. With the aid of Alfred Hitchcock and John Buchan, a few primitive location shots, and a misty recreation of the Highlands – a cardboard bridge, some hired sheep – 'The Thirty Nine Steps' triumphed. It may have dumped Buchan's plot but it substituted a neat tale of cat-and-mouse, which allowed Robert Donat to encounter cool Madeleine Carroll. As an advert for the romance of Scotland it is unsurpassed.

'The Ghost Goes West' also took a fresh look at the Scottish stereotype, this time for laughs. Donat played both Donald and Murdoch Glourie, one the impoverished laird, the other the cursed ghostly ancestor who merrily haunts Eugene Pallette and family when they buy castle Korda and transport it to Florida.

Michael Powell was looking for a different kind of Scottish drama and found it in 'Edge Of The World'. filmed on Foula and based on the evacuation of St Kilda, it was strikingly different from the studio productions of the time. This was not a whimsical tale of kilties, but a dark drama of life and death in an isolated community. Powell was too much of an artist to rely on a documentary style (then considered superior to any fiction), but his location work – with its cliffs, storms, and seagulls – provided a haunting backdrop to the actors.

While Hollywood Scots tended to be minor, though much-used, players – like Andy Clyde from 'Hopalong Cassidy' or Mary Gordon, spectacularly despatched in 'Bride Of Frankenstein' – the British studios had stars to employ. Will Fyffe, for example, moved his stage persona onto the screen and emerged a fine character actor. In 'Owd Bob', strangely set in Cumberland, he was the canny Scots shepherd, and in 'Rulers Of The Sea' Fyffe was the drunken inventor racing to cross the Atlantic. The very different Jack Buchanan similarly widened his success by taking to the screen, but his suave talent was that of the international sophisticate rather than a son of Helensburgh.

129

HOLLYWOOD IRISH AS NORTHWEST FRONTIER SCOT – VICTOR MCLAGLEN DEFENDS THE EMPIRE IN 'WEE WILLIE WINKIE', 1937.

FROM MGM TO EALING

Propaganda thrills and good spirits were the main points for wartime productions, so Powell and partner Emeric Pressburger looked up north again and came up with 'The Spy In Black', a Great War spy yarn atmospherically set in a studio recreation of Hoy, an island conveniently shrouded in fog. With a plot involving an honourable U-boat Commander, a comic minister, and an island schoolmistress who was not what she seemed (as one might have guessed from Valerie Hobson's grand manner), it is a charming film, if not the last word on Orcadian culture.

Scotland bobbed up with less conviction and certainly less artistry in a number of other British features. Most people were chasing spies in remote spots: Leslie Banks was mysterious in a 'Cottage To Let', Will Hay's bumbling hit Skye in 'The Ghost Of St Michael's', and Arthur Askey probed a lighthouse in 'Back Room Boy'. Clive Brook was up Clydeside way in 'The Shipbuilders'. In Cronin's 'Hatters Castle', Robert Newton was the domineering father of lovely Deborah Kerr; alcoholic, crafty and cunning. Across the North Sea the German film industry chose this time to present Mary Queen of Scots to the world once more, as enemy of the English, in the person of Zarah Leander.

In Hollywood, busy making pictures to cheer up the world, 'British' films had never been more popular. There were no Scots epics, however, to compare with 'How Green Was My Valley', although Donald Crisp won an Oscar playing Welsh, and the rest of the cast seemed to consist of Los Angeles' Irish community. MGM, however, seems to have had a fondness for the nation. On screen, courtesy of Metro, there was a misty posting for the Air Force lovers in 'A Guy Named Joe' – Spencer Tracy and Irene Dunne found a warm log fire, but no natives. For Vivien Leigh in 'Waterloo Bridge',

Scotland was a world of formal balls and snobbish in-laws. And the old music hall stereotype gave Hollywood's Best Actress of 1942 a chance to display her legs as opposed to her gentle nobility. Greer Garson flirts briefly with tartanry in 'Random Harvest'. Just after she has found amnesiac Ronald Colman wandering in the fog, she has to do her turn on stage. Not for her a yearning ballad: here she is in mini-kilt impersonating Harry Lauder for 'She's Ma Daisy'. It drives the soldiers wild, and poor Colman collapses. This was not what we expected from Mrs Miniver.

It was a time when Crisp or Edmund Gwenn or Dame May Witty could pass for any British type, California could be any part of Scotland, only sunnier, and a fetching collie could be a star. In her/his debut feature 'Lassie Come Home' the star is taken off by a well-meaning Nigel Bruce to the Highlands. Despite the kind words of a violet-eyed doll (a ten-year-old Elizabeth Taylor), Lassie escapes and sets off on an epic trek, through the Rockies it seems, to find Roddy McDowall in Yorkshire. Scotland never looked lovelier, the cottages and natives never cuter. And the Technicolor was glorious. The canine star returned to MGM's Scotland for further dramatic roles in 'The Hills Of Home', and notably as Greyfriars Bobby in 'Challenge To Lassie'. It may be easy to scoff now, but the supporting casts were top-notch (if familiar – Gwenn, Crisp and so on again) and Metro had made an effort to get Edinburgh's Old Town looking right in Culver City.

Hollywood saw Scotland as a good standby for a creepy thriller or a colourful swashbuckler. RKO gamely tackled R L Stevenson's 'The Bodysnatcher' as part of its series of low-budget shockers, creating an evocative foggy Edinburgh as it recast the Burke and Hare story with Karloff and Lugosi. Henry Daniell elegantly played a version of Dr Knox's anatomist, and despite lapses in the costuming it had an authentic Gothic feel.

At Columbia there was a return to the plaid-ridden Scotland of the silent days. Larry Parks, briefly a screen favourite after 'The Jolson Story',

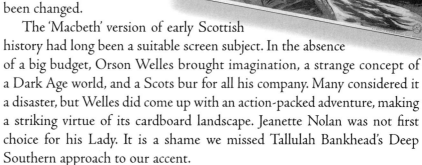

found himself invading Errol Flynn and Cornel Wilde territory as 'The Swordsman'. Set amongst feuding Highland clans, the Glowans and the MacArdens, this was supposed to be a true story. Studio publicity suggested only the names and tartans had been changed.

The 'Macbeth' version of early Scottish history had long been a suitable screen subject. In the absence of a big budget, Orson Welles brought imagination, a strange concept of a Dark Age world, and a Scots bur for all his company. Many considered it a disaster, but Welles did come up with an action-packed adventure, making a striking virtue of its cardboard landscape. Jeanette Nolan was not first choice for his Lady. It is a shame we missed Tallulah Bankhead's Deep Southern approach to our accent.

As World War II ended, there was an outburst of Scottish romance, strangely not from Hollywood which was discovering *film noir* and the psychological drama, but from Powell and Pressburger once more, with 'I Know Where I'm Going'. It is ironic that their original choice for leading-lady was Deborah Kerr. Had she played it – and in colour as originally planned – we would have had a red-haired Scottish actress playing an English girl, with dark, brooding James Mason as the Laird of Kiloran. As it turned out, the Technicolor stock was in short supply and delays meant we had charming substitutes in Wendy Hiller and red-headed Roger Livesey, all in black and white.

But what beautiful black and white. Filmed on Mull without Livesey, who was in London, but with every ounce of the Powell/Pressburger talent, it brought a Scotland – and specifically a 'Western Isles' – to the screen which was fresh yet ancient, real yet mystical. Wendy Hiller's practical working girl sets out for wealth, goes astray in bad weather, meets a laird on a jetty and finds love. There was singing, Finlay Currie, Tobermory, a bit of Gaelic, an old curse, some Highland cattle and a ceilidh. How could it fail? A little further up the coast Patricia Roc was in very good company indeed in 'The Brothers' in 1947, showing that costume drama was not only Gainsborough romance. A strong cast of Finlay Currie, Will Fyffe, Duncan Macrae and John Laurie pulled out all the stops in this grim poetic tragedy set on Skye. The Cuillins made an impressive background to David Macdonald's film of family treachery and violence stirred up by the appearance of an orphaned convent girl in a low-cut bodice.

But the challenge of bringing a major historical figure to the screen would fall to the great romantic of British films, Alexander Korda. He had long wanted to bring the Jacobites to the screen, and had toyed with Donat or Leslie Howard for the Young Pretender – or indeed the Old Pretender – throughout the 1930s. With their romantic persona it might just have worked, but by 1947 when 'Bonnie Prince Charlie' became a post-war reality, there was nothing but trouble. Directors changed, Will Fyffe died, and the authentic clashing tartans dismayed the designer. Some German accents, a brandy bottle, and the inexplicable presence of Clementina Walkinshaw were signs of authenticity. For the most part, however, it was jewel-bright colour, pretty scenery, Jacobite ballads, and a plot which failed to thrill. A clean-shaven, yellow-haired David Niven was not quite the Prince, either of legend or reality, and the fact he was Scottish-born was neither here nor there. Margaret Leighton, that starry Shaftesbury Avenue confection, was Flora MacDonald. Clearly the timing was off, or Korda's magic was no longer weaving its spell.

Ealing Studios, however, captured an alternative version of Scottish life round about the same time. Joan Greenwood got to play the postmaster's daughter with a witchery all of her own in 'Whisky Galore!', Alexander MacKendrick's sly version of the Compton Mackenzie novel. With location filming on Barra, this story of whisky lost and found and islanders outwitting English superior Basil Radford looked and felt like the real thing, and there was a cast to savour – with Duncan Macrae back in comedy and a lovely duo of mother and son from Gordon Jackson and Jean Cadell. It set the pattern for future Scottish films – if we were not being romantic we would be canny, quaint and original.

For director David Lean 'Madeleine' was an act of love for his then wife Ann Todd, a cool blonde beauty who did not affect a Scottish accent for her role as the young Miss Smith famous for being Not Proven. The production boasted trips down the Clyde and an excellent recreation of Victorian Glasgow and Edinburgh – while the drama unfolded of the French lover who may or may not have been poisoned by the demure lady of the title. Scots turned up in support in another Victorian setting, when Finlay Currie (shortly to play St Peter in 'Quo Vadis?' and later King David in 'Solomon and Sheba') brought his fine beard and native wit to the role of John Brown in 'The Mudlark'. This was opposite Irene Dunne's Victoria; her usual formidable charm smothered by the required padding. Irishman Richard Todd garnered an Oscar nomination for his dour dying Scots soldier in 'The Hasty Heart', and there was not a dry eye in the house as Patricia Neal saw to it that his last hospital days in Burma were warm and loved. He was soon to become the screen's favourite Scot. Bridie's 'The Sleeping Clergyman' came to the screen with Todd, as did 'Flesh And Blood'. A generation-spanning Glasgow medical drama, it also allowed Joan Greenwood to do her Scots minx again, and there was Glynis Johns too.

'Happy Go Lovely' was something peculiar. A British musical with a Betty Grable director and co-star, an MGM dancer, and David Niven, set at the Edinburgh Festival. Vera-Ellen had only lately been going 'On The Town', but the Athens of the North was frugal with its charms. Such tartan frolics were not below greater stars either. When Astaire and Rogers returned in 'The Barkeleys Of Broadway' a Scottish number was thrown in, along with Ginger's rendition of 'La Marseillaise'. MGM was broad-minded. But it could also get away with it.

What can have been more different from a lacklustre imitation of Hollywood than laudable attempts by small British companies to make worthwhile Scottish drama? The aim: to put on the screen a recognisable people and society. 'Worthy' rather than 'sensational' was the verdict, but at least 'Floodtide' put a real Clydeside on record. Gordon Jackson was the apprentice who falls in love with the boss's daughter, Rona Anderson, supported by a familiar array of Scottish talent including Jimmy Logan and John Laurie. 'The Gorbals Story' came from a notable play, but the transformation to the screen took away much of the pungency and humour of the original. A strong cast remained, including Russell Hunter and Roddy Macmillan, and a fascinating – if muted, and no doubt uncommercial – glimpse of a time and a place.

The early 1950s brought widely different features from John Grierson, the famed documentary film-maker. 'You're Only Young Twice' was another Bridie adaptation; a farce set in Glasgow University, with Duncan Macrae and some capable comedy players. But 'The Brave Don't Cry', which may have sounded like a Joan Crawford vehicle, was something of a success. A stark drama set in an Ayrshire mining community, with 100 trapped far below ground, it was both recognisably Scottish, yet international in its theme. How different from 'Laxdale Hall'. Here was more Ealing territory, filmed in Applecross, and the usual tale of wily locals and hapless outsiders, but full of fun and, as always, well acted by a familiar cast. (For the American market, it was the rather more enticing 'Scotch On The Rocks'.)

137

THE BRIGADOON YEARS

Hollywood was in love with Scotland once more, and in the 1950s, as many American productions sought out colourful locations all over the world, we benefited from some notable visitors intent on capturing the Highlands and the heather on the big screen. How could British companies compete with the sheer nerve of these swashbucklers? There was even talk of Hedy Lamarr following her Delilah with Mary Stuart.

'The Master Of Ballantrae' was a great Stevenson tale, though Warner Brothers chose to replace the plot with their own. By 1953 Errol Flynn had been fencing for them for nearly 20 years and his face and figure were beginning to fail – so that he and Anthony Steel made an odd pair of brothers: one suitably dour, the other more than a touch of the roué. Nevertheless it made a spirited adventure – Ballantrae was fetchingly played by Eilean Donan, and there were a lot of cockades, bonnets and trews. The darkness of Stevenson's original was lost to full-blooded Technicolor and Roger Livesey's scene-stealing. The 1745 was reduced to a montage of flags and drums.

For 'Rob Roy – The Highland Rogue' – we got the 1715 and a lot of Titian beards. Richard Todd was called into service once more for his Celtic accent, as was Glynis Johns, with James Robertson Justice. Walt Disney was the producer. It was never intended to be a grand period recreation, or even a version of Scott, and so it proved. But what a fine figure of a hero Todd made.

1954 was a remarkable, some might say infamous, year for Scotland and film. In Hollywood MGM brought Lerner and Loewe's Scottish fantasy 'Brigadoon' to the screen. Producer Arthur Freed had scouted for locations in Scotland, but had rejected them all. The country he wanted was created in Culver City, with designs that merited an Oscar nomination. Vincente

139

MARGARET LOCKWOOD, THE WICKED LADY LAIRD, CONFRONTS VICTOR MCLAGLEN'S KING OF THE TINKERS – DEFINITELY 'TROUBLE IN THE GLEN', 1954. (EDINBURGH FILM GUILD)

Minnelli had already made St Louis for Garland, Paris for Gene Kelly; he would soon recreate Baghdad for Kismet – so why not the Highlands? A lot of great talents were involved in 'Brigadoon', yet it is usually thought that something went a little awry in the telling, despite the beauty of the songs, the dancing, and Cyd Charisse. As the zenith of Scottish kitsch, its place in cinema history is secure.

Meanwhile in Britain, two Herberts – Mr Yates of Republic Pictures, and Mr Wilcox, long-time presenter of Anna Neagle – were creating a follow up to 'The Quiet Man'. With another novel by Maurice Walsh as its source, they hoped 'Trouble In The Glen' would repeat that Oscar winner's success. Orson Welles was the new laird, Forrest Tucker was in the John Wayne role as the visiting American, Margaret Lockwood was the spirited lady, Victor McLaglen was the king of the tinkers, and a crippled lassie was thrown in for sympathy value. Lacking a decent plot, it might have got by on charm and scenic beauty. It had neither – all suffered at the hands of Trucolor. Trouble in the glen indeed.

Strangely enough, there was another Scottish rural drama going the rounds at the same time, also with little children, and even a charming baby, but this was set in Nova Scotia. Philip Leacock's 'The Kidnappers', filmed in Glen Affric, was a remarkable world-wide success. Duncan Macrae was the stern patriarch of the Scottish community in Cape Breton; Jean Anderson and Adrienne Corri were his family. Jon Whitely and Vincent Winter as the little boys who crave a dog but steal a baby instead won special Oscars.

Making the journey back across the Atlantic was Paul Douglas, a robust Hollywood star in the Spencer Tracy mould, who came to claim a peach of a part in 'The Maggie'. Alexander MacKendrick wove a spirited comedy for his Scottish cast, and the Ealing yarn of an aged puffer and an exasperated American showed the West Coast to advantage. Not for the first or last time we would see Scotland's transformation skills on a hard-boiled outsider. This time, however, the puffer's crew – Alexander Mackenzie *et al* – would be a mite less obviously charming than Miss Charisse. The script and direction had an edge, and the scenery was appealing without leaning towards the postcard picturesque.

Just as Richard Todd gave another interpretation of his widescreen Scotsman – this time as 'A Man Called Peter', the minister who got to the top in America, there was another claimant to the title of favourite screen Scot – Bill Travers as 'Geordie'. A slight Launder and Gilliat comedy, full of colour and character, it told the story of the wee lad who buys into Charles Atlas and gets to the Olympics. Alastair Sim was the laird, and Travers got to be a porridge advert come to life. It was such a success that the same team put together another slice of Highland life for 'The Bridal Path'. This time Travers was the Hebridean on the loose in Oban looking for a wife. Lots of Gaelic songs, and lots of scenery. Like its predecessor, it was entirely lacking in pretension, all very jolly and agreeable – and at least the landscape, like a Tourist Board advert, was real.

141

Sequels and remakes were the thing in the late 1950s. 'Rockets Galore!' was a return to a familiar Hebridean island, where a military base rather than whisky was the bone of contention. The same old reliable team from Scottish Equity was assembled, along with Donald Sinden and Roland Culver as the obligatory invading English, but this time colour allowed us to see the pivotal hue of the seagulls – for plot purposes, pink. Kenneth More was the hero running along the Forth Bridge in the new 'Thirty Nine Steps', which found little favour anywhere despite its breezy leading man, and the genuine location work which the original had lacked. But a new 'Kidnapped', a further example of Walt Disney's affection for Scotland, came up trumps. With an old-time director in Robert Stevenson, a cast of genuine stalwarts, the glamorous Peter Finch as Breck, and the surprising but successful casting of James MacArthur (hadn't his mother Helen Hayes been a great J M Barrie star?), it stuck to Stevenson's story and set it all against an authentic backdrop.

BILL TRAVERS IS SEEN
OFF TO THE OLYMPICS
BY HIS HAPPY FELLOW
HIGHLANDERS IN
'GEORDIE', 1955.
(EDINBURGH FILM GUILD)

Then there were more Disney projects – 'Greyfriars Bobby', with bits of real Edinburgh, gave Donald Crisp one of his last leading roles as the kirkyard keeper at Greyfriars. Finlay Currie was one of the authentic humans in the Inverary locations of 'The Three Lives Of Thomasina'. Warner Brothers did not seek out Kirkbean on the Solway when John Farrow constructed his epic on the founder of the US Navy, 'John Paul Jones'. Perhaps the charm of the reality was lost on the studio; instead they created a Brigadoon-type village, swirling with bagpipes, for Robert Stack's birthplace.

But Scotland was better served by, of all things, a James Thurber comedy, when Constance Cummings and Peter Sellars took on 'The Battle Of The Sexes'. Cummings was the American expert eager to make a long-established Tweed firm a mite more efficient, and Sellars was the faithful clerk who tries to sabotage her efforts, and then her abrasive self. Sellars caught the Auld Reekie accent to a tee, and under Charles Crichton's skilled comedy direction, the location filming and character support shone.

Stirling Castle and an identifiable tartan were faked for the film of James Kennaway's 'Tunes Of Glory' when the subject matter of the film proved too delicate for the Army. A Mess drama of warring Colonels, featuring alcohol, madness and suicide, it cast Alec Guinness and John Mills in the leads, with Duncan Macrae (inevitably), Gordon Jackson and John Fraser on hand to show how the words should really sound. A bitter but unexpected melodrama, there was an Oscar nomination for Kennaway's screenplay. More in keeping with the usual cosy view was 'The Amorous Prawn', a West End comedy with purring Joan Greenwood as a hard-up Colonel's wife making the most of her Highland assets.

Stars could go south too, as Stanley Baxter showed in Rank's 'The Fast Lady'. Here he was as leading man, bashful Scot perhaps, but transformed to roadhog and hero – and the winner of Julie Christie, a mere three years before international fame and Omar Sharif claimed her. 'Carry On Up The Khyber' recalled the glory days of the Black Watch, but there was more

143

prestigious campery in 'The Prime Of Miss Jean Brodie'. As Muriel Spark's famous creation, Maggie Smith got to trot her gels round some of Edinburgh's more photogenic sights, in a curious 1960s version of the 1930s. Celia Johnson was the surprise – it was a joy to hear her switch the familiar Coward tones for Morningside, and she was a sharp piece of work as the Headmistress.

There was always scenery to enjoy in Scottish films – 'The Private Life Of Sherlock Holmes' took Robert Stephens to Loch Ness, and an older Bill Travers was back in the Highlands. This time he was playing about with otters in 'Ring Of Bright Water', a family film which, charm aside, had nothing to do with the real Gavin Maxwell. There were stranger goings on in the Borders. Roddy McDowall, erstwhile child star and master of Lassie, arrived in Ettrick to film 'Tam Lin' in authentic locations. The old ballad was reset in the swinging 1960s, with Ian McShane as the lad spirited away by the fairies, and Stephanie Beacham as the fair Janet, here a minister's daughter, who tries to save him. A strange choice for a cinema project, but one graced by a genuine star, queening it from Traquair, swathed in Balmain – the wicked lady was Ava Gardner. An oddity, beautifully filmed, and catching at the poetry of folklore.

Galloway's turn came with 'The Wicker Man'. Edward Woodward was the poor bobby investigating a disappearance, and finding more than he bargained for. In the great tradition of 'I Know Where I'm Going' and 'Brigadoon', he was the outsider transformed by local values – but this time he ended up as human sacrifice, not settling down with a dancing beauty or red-haired laird. 'The Wicker Man' was a heady brew of matter-of-fact pagan ritual and cheery songs. An original certainly.

More routine fare was on offer too – another version of 'Kidnapped' with the odd casting of Michael Caine as Alan Breck, plus a gallery of sterling support, 1950s vintage. 'Macbeth' burst onto the screen again with Polanski's robust Jon Finch and Francesca Annis as the young couple, now

THEY KISSED ON THE FORTH BRIDGE, THEY ESCAPED INTO THE MIST, AND NOW THEY ARE HANDCUFFED TOGETHER IN A COUNTRY PUB.
MADELEINE CARROLL AND ROBERT DONAT IN 'THE THIRTY-NINE STEPS', 1935. (EDINBURGH FILM GUILD)

domiciled in the castles of Northumberland. Bette Davis was to be spotted in Tobermory as the evil genius of 'Madam Sin'. Robert Powell got to be the new Richard Hannay, racing over authentic Dumfriesshire moors in a production that took 'The Thirty-Nine Steps' back to 1914, and its lead from Buchan rather than Hitchcock. Powell may have been Jesus, but Donat was beyond him.

'Mary Queen of Scots' was not quite as dramatic as it should have been, though Vanessa Redgrave's pale golden blonde sang a sweet song, rode in drag, and won an Oscar nomination. In the 1960s there had been ambitious talk of an authentically Gallic-accented lady, perhaps Catherine Deneuve, in an Alexander MacKendrick film which would strip away the myths. What we did get was an old-style Hollywood picture from an old-style Hollywood producer. Hermitage Castle was the sole authentic location. Nigel Davenport was Bothwell, Ian Holm was Rizzio and Timothy Dalton was Darnley.

While Redgrave and company were being painstakingly costumed and lit for Universal's epic, Bill Douglas was creating the first of his trilogy: 'My Childhood', soon to be followed by 'My Ain Folk' and then 'My Way Home'. Douglas's work was the very antithesis of the commercial offerings that usually put Scotland on screen. Grim and grainy recreations of a hard childhood in a mining community and adolescence in an institution; filmed with skill but none of the comforting artifice of Hollywood, they created haunting images of pain and love – but it was not perhaps for a world audience.

Bill Forsyth, on the other hand, brought the audiences in with his Cumbernauld comedy 'Gregory's Girl'. Looking like real life, but a coyly innocent one, its Scots hero was lanky and anything but heroic. Given its success however, the drollery must have been understood round the world. 'Chariots Of Fire' looked back reassuringly at the old Empire days, with a little contemporary thinking added, and a soaring score. Only partly a

Scottish drama, the Edinburgh and St Andrews locations made cunning settings for some of the English scenes. Ian Charleson was the running missionary, and it was all bathed in the golden light of nostalgia.

A starker view of the past was on offer in 'Another Time, Another Place'. Jessie Kesson's honest account of the Black Isle in wartime, with Phyllis Logan as the lonely farmer's wife falling for the mischievous – but certainly not glamorous – charms of an Italian POW. It was far from a conventional romance, taking no comfort from period settings or landscape.

In any case, what audience wanted to see isolation and bad weather on screen when Bill Forsyth could serve up fare which had gone down very well in the past? 'Local Hero' was his most ambitious effort yet – a return it seemed to the Ealing days. Certainly all the elements were there: picturesque settings, quirky locals, a visiting star, and a smear or two of Celtic romanticism – but perhaps the schoolboy jokes and the dollops of charm were misjudged. Or perhaps all those things just were more at home in 1954. However, it was a great success. Forsyth then whipped up 'Comfort And Joy', a wee confection concerning Glasgow's ice-cream wars, before the much less charming reality echoed 'The Godfather'.

At least there was spectacle in 'Highlander', a crazy adventure of wizardry over the centuries. Christopher Lambert was the warrior who finds he is immortal. He poses heroically in Glencoe, and in a bit of cheeky casting Sean Connery is not a Scot. This was Lambert's second screen visit to Scotland. A few years before, the ancestral pile of Lord Greystoke – aka Tarzan of the Apes – had been identified as Floors Castle at Kelso. No great play was made of the apeman's Scottish ancestry, but there was a ghillies' ball. Connery, of course, is Scotland's great gift to the cinema world. But like Deborah Kerr before him, he has rarely been distinctively Scottish on screen, probably for sound commercial reasons, and it was as an Irishman that he won his Oscar.

... AND FINALLY

On screen as the 1980s ended, there was Barlinnie in David Hayman's striking 'Silent Scream'; Stromness in 'Venus Peter'; and Barra airport in 'Play Me Something'. Scotland again as that strange country of contrasts, this time courtesy of British film Institute funding. Handsome films, but not blockbusters. But the last decade of the century would mark an unexpected upsurge in films from Scotland – there would be the return of an old favourite, some cheeky drug-takers, and one small hero with a big voice and a huge influence.

'The Big Man' looked like a bid for international success from the start, with William McIlvanney's novel given an operatic treatment and a score by Ennio Morricone – no grim television drama this but a major feature with a big star. Liam Neeson followed the great tradition of Richard Todd as a world-class attraction. And then there was a nasty tale of three not very appealing young citizens who find a rich corpse in their spare bedroom. 'Shallow Grave' had a striking version of an Edinburgh flat, and Ewan McGregor became a star. And then from the same team there was 'Trainspotting'; a different version of Scotland – the grim desolation of urban life. A drug comedy-drama with non-stop action, it had a pungent collection of young actors and a pulsating soundtrack. The landscape this time was bleak, the actions far from heroic, but the star quality on show was genuinely home-grown.

1995 was the big year for the Scottish hero and the Scottish landscape. The mountains were real, but the stars were foreign. Liam Neeson was first to make his bow with 'Rob Roy', in a handsome film written and directed by Scots: Michael Caton-Jones and Alan Sharp. Rather earthier than Disney's version, it still knew when to rely on the beauties of the landscape.

Much was made of the idea that this was simply a Western in kilts – a selling point. 'Rob Roy's' thunder was somewhat overshadowed by 'Braveheart', Mel Gibson's directorial debut, with the star himself as William Wallace. With a plot that might have done for Alan Ladd and Virginia Mayo, it had little to do with history, and artistically not enough to do with 'Spartacus' or 'El Cid'. Audiences loved it throughout the world and it won the Best Picture Oscar. In Scotland it ran and ran, which was the surprise. Perhaps audiences were hungry for an old-fashioned historical epic and did not mind the liberties taken with fact. Gibson's face, painted blue and white, became a modern icon, and in cinemas there was spontaneous applause.

Scotland was certainly back on screen in a big way as the century ended. Scenery, history and urban decay – we had them all. Hollywood dropped by for 'Loch Ness', relocating Eilean Donan for scenic purposes, and finding a local lassie to charm the beastie. The Bruce rode up to be counted in a small way. Lars Von Trier brought poetry to the oil rigs with 'Breaking The Waves'. Ken Loach visited Glasgow for 'Carla's Song' with Robert Carlyle and 'My Name Is Joe' with Peter Mullan. Scots were well to the fore – Gillies MacKinnon recreated 1960s Glasgow with photogenic young Scots in 'Small Faces', and then went back to the trenches of World War I for 'Regeneration'. Judi Dench and Billy Connolly played in 'Mrs Brown'. Peter Mullan's 'Orphans' caused a stir, and Lynne Ramsay's 'Ratcatcher' won awards.

A hundred years of cinema, and where are we? A small and distinctive nation, with noted talents on both sides of the camera. We started the century as a music hall joke, and ended it as a symbol of rugged independence.

SCOTLAND ON THE BIG SCREEN:
SELECTED FEATURE FILMS

THE AMOROUS PRAWN (1962)
Director: Anthony Kimmins
With: Joan Greenwood, Ian Carmichael, Cecil Parker, Dennis Price
Bored lady laird fools tourists.

ANNIE LAURIE (1927)
Director: John S Robertson
With: Lillian Gish, Norman Kerry,Creighton Hale, Hobart Boswoth, David Torrence
Feuding clans, frail star.

ANOTHER TIME, ANOTHER PLACE (1983)
Director: Michael Radford
With: Phyllis Logan, Gian Luca Favilla, Paul Young, Tom Watson, Denise Coffey
Lonely wife falls for Italian POW.

AULD ROBIN GREY (1910)
Director: Larry Trimble
With: Florence Turner, Maurice Costello
But she gets the young one in the end.

BATTLE OF THE SEXES (1959)
Director: Charles Crichton
With: Peter Sellers, Constance Cummings, Robert Morley
Edinburgh firm faces American dragon.

BESIDE THE BONNIE BRIAR BUSH (1921)
Director: Donald Crisp
With: Donald Crisp, Mary Glynne
Kailyard meets Hollywood.

THE BIG MAN (1990)
Director: David Leland
With: Liam Neeson, Joanne Whalley-Kilmer, Billy Connolly, Ian Bannen, Maurice Roeves
Boxer goes for the big-time.

THE BIG TEASE (1999)
Director: Kevin Allen
With: Craig Ferguson, Frances Fisher, Chris Langham, Mary McCormack
Hairdresser hits Hollywood.

BILLY TWO HATS (1973)
Director: Ted Kotcheff
With: Gregory Peck, Desi Arnez jnr, Jack Warden, David Huddleston
Scots cowboy in old West.

THE BODYSNATCHER (1946)
Director: Robert Wise
With: Henry Daniell, Boris Karloff, Bela Lugosi, Edith Atwater
Burke and Hare in Old Town Hollywood.

BONNIE PRINCE CHARLIE (1923)
Director: C C Calvert
With: Ivor Novello, Gladys Cooper
Bonnie certainly.

BONNIE PRINCE CHARLIE (1947)
Director: Anthony Kimmins
With: David Niven, Margaret Leighton, Jack Hawkins, Judy Campbell, Finlay Currie, John Laurie
Defeated.

BONNIE SCOTLAND (1935)
Director: James W Horne
With: Stan Laurel, Oliver Hardy, June Lang, Daphne Pollard, David Torrence
Duo seek inheritance, end up in India.

THE BRAVE DON'T CRY (1952)
Director: Philip Leacock
With: John Gregson, Meg Buchanan, John Rae, Fulton Mackay, Andrew Keir
Grim drama of trapped miners.

BRAVEHEART (1995)
Director: Mel Gibson
With: Mel Gibson, Angus MacFadyen, Ian Bannen, Patrick McGoohan, Sophie Marceau, Catherine McCormack, Brian Cox, Peter Mullan, James Cosmo
Wee star makes big hero.

BREAKING THE WAVES (1996)
Director: Lars Von Trier
With: Emily Watson, Stellan Skarsgard, Katrin Cartlidge, Jean-Marc Barr, Adrian Rawlins, Udo Kier
Simple lass finds love, almost loses love, saves love.

THE BRIDAL PATH (1959)
Director: Frank Launder
With: Bill Travers, Bernadette O' Farrell, George Cole, Gordon Jackson, Duncan Macrae
Strapping islander seek wife on mainland.

THE BRIDE OF LAMMERMOOR (1909)
Director: J Stuart Blackton
With: Annette Kellerman, Maurice Costello
Swimming star plays Lucia.

BRIGADOON (1954)
Director: Vincente Minnelli
With: Gene Kelly, Van Johnson, Cyd Charisse, Elaine Stewart, Barry Jones, Hugh Laing
American tourists trip over enchanted village.

THE BROTHERS (1947)
Director: David MacDonald
With: Patricia Roc, Will Fyffe, Maxwell Reed, Finlay Currie, Duncan Macrae, John Laurie
Servant girls stirs up Skye families.

THE BRUCE (1996)
Director: Bob Carruthers, David McWhinnie *With:* Oliver Reed, Brian Blessed, Sandy Welch, Hildegard Neil, Conor Chamberlain
Small-scale version of wars of independence.

BUNTY PULLS THE STRINGS (1921)
Director: Reginald Barker
With: Leatrice Joy, Russell Simpson, Raymond Hatton
Elder's daughter does just that.

CARLA'S SONG (1996)
Director: Ken Loach *With:* Robert Carlyle, Oyanka Cabezas, Scott Glenn, Salvador Espinoza, Louise Goodall
Glasgow bus driver encounters Nicaragua.

CHALLENGE TO LASSIE (1949)
Director: Richard Thorpe
With: Lassie, Edmund Gwenn, Donald Crisp, Reginald Owen, Sara Allgood, Henry Stephenson
Collie plays Greyfriars Bobby.

CHARIOTS OF FIRE (1981)
Director: Hugh Hudson
With: Ian Charleson, Ben Cross, Nigel Havers, Nicholas Farrell, Cheryl Campbell, Nigel Davenport, Ian Holm
Scots missionary runs the Olympics.

CHASING THE DEER (1994)
Director: Graham Holloway
With: Brian Blessed, Iain Cuthbertson, Matthew Zajac, Fish, Brian Donald
Jacobites without the songs.

COMFORT AND JOY (1984)
Director: Bill Forsyth
With: Bill Paterson, Eleanor David, C P Grogan, Alex Norton, Patrick Malahide
Ice-cream intrigue.

COMPLICITY (2000)
Director: Gavin Millar *With:* Jonny Lee Miller, Valerie Edmond, Keely Hawes
Journalist threatened in popular novel.

COUNTRY DANCE (1971)
Director: J Lee Thompson
With: Peter O'Toole, Susannah York, Michael Craig, Harry Andrews
Highland family get too close.

DEATH WATCH (LA MORT EN DIRECT) (1979)
Director: Bertrand Tavernier
With: Romy Schneider, Harvey Keitel, Harry Dean Stanton, Max Von Sydow, Robbie Coltrane
Futuristic Glasgow thriller.

THE DEBT COLLECTOR (1999)
Director: Anthony Nielson
With: Billy Connolly, Francesca Annis, Ken Stott, Iain Robertson, Annette Crosbie
Shady dealings in underworld.

DEVIL GIRL FROM MARS (1954)
Director: David MacDonald
With: Patricia Laffan, Hugh McDermott, Joseph Tomelty, Adrienne Corri, Hazel Court, John Laurie
Queen of Mars seeks Scots studs.

THE DOCTOR AND THE DEVILS (1985)
Director: Freddie Francis
With: Timothy Dalton, Twiggy, Jonathan Pryce
Burke and Hare again.

THE EDGE OF THE WORLD (1937)
Director: Michael Powell
With: John Laurie, Belle Chrystall, Eric Berry, Finlay Currie, Nial MacGinnis
Harsh island life, Foula plays St Kilda.

EYE OF THE NEEDLE (1981)
Director: Richard Marquand
With: Donald Sutherland, Kate Nelligan, Christopher Cazenove, Ian Bannen
Nazi spy on Scottish island.

FLESH AND BLOOD (1951)
Director: Anthony Kimmins
With: Richard Todd, Glynis Johns, Joan Greenwood, André Morell, Ursula Howells, Freda Jackson
Three Glasgow generations in Bridie adaptation.

FLOOD TIDE (1949)
Director: Frederick Wilson
With: Gordon Jackson, Rona Anderson, John Laurie, Jack Lambert
Working class boy wins boss's daughter.

FOOTBALL DAFT (1921)
Director: Victor Rowe
With: Jimmy Brough
Glasgow comedy.

GEORDIE (1955)
Director: Frank Launder
With: Alastair Sim, Bill Travers, Paul Young, Norah Gorsen, Anna Ferguson
Highland lad grows up big and strong.

THE GHOST GOES WEST (1935)
Director: Rene Clair *With:* Robert Donat, Jean Parker, Eugene Pallette, Hay Petrie
Impoverished laird sells haunted castle.

THE GIRL IN THE PICTURE (1986)
Director: Cary Parker *With:* John Gordon Sinclair, Irina Brook, David MacKay, Gregor Fisher, Caroline Guthrie
Gangly youth in love, again.

THE GORBALS STORY (1950)
Director: David MacKane
With: Russell Hunter, Archie Duncan, Roddy Macmillan, Betty Henderson, Howard Connell
Tenement life, almost real.

GREGORY'S GIRL (1980)
Director: Bill Forsyth
With: John Gordon Sinclair, Dee Hepburn, Jake D'Arcy, Claire Grogan, Robert Buchanan
First love in a New Town.

GREGORY'S TWO GIRLS (1999)
Director: Bill Forsyth
With: John Gordon Sinclair, Dougray Scott, Maria Doyle Kennedy, Fiona Bell
Grown man, still in tangles.

GREYFRIARS BOBBY (1960)
Director: Don Chaffey
With: Donald Crisp, Laurence Naismith, Alexander Mackenzie, Kay Walsh, Andrew Cruickshank
Faithful terrier, free dog of city.

HAPPY GO LOVELY (1950)
Director: Bruce Humberstone
With: Vera-Ellen, David Niven, Cesar Romero
An Edinburgh Festival musical?

THE HARP KING (1919)
Director: Max Leder
With: Nan Wilkie, David Watt, WR Bell
Unsuitable musician suitor.

THE HASTY HEART (1949)
Director: Vincent Sherman
With: Richard Todd, Ronald Reagan, Patricia Neal
Buddies warm to dour dying Scot.

HATTER'S CASTLE (1941)
Director: Lance Comfort
With: Robert Newton, Deborah Kerr, Emlyn Williams
Tyrannical Victorian father.

THE HEART OF MIDLOTHIAN (1914)
Director: Frank Wilson *With:* Flora Morris, Violet Hopson, Alma Taylor
A version of Scott.

HEAVENLY PURSUITS (1986)
Director: Charles Gormley
With: Tom Conti, Helen Mirren
Miracles in Glasgow.

HIGHLANDER (1986)
Director: Russell Mulcahy
With: Christopher Lambert, Sean Connery, Roxanne Hart
Time-bending hero fights evil.

HILLS OF HOME (1948)
Director: Fred Wilcox
With: Lassie, Edmund Gwenn, Tom Drake, Donald Crisp, Janet Leigh
Doctor and dog come home.

HUNTED (1952)
Director: Charles Crichton
With: Dirk Bogarde, Jon Whitely, Kay Walsh, Elizabeth Sellars
Rank star and Scots tot on the run.

HUNTINGTOWER (1927)
Director: George Pearson
With: Harry Lauder, Vera Vororina, Pat Aherne, Nancy Price
Buchan comedy-thriller.

I KNOW WHERE I'M GOING (1944)
Director: Michael Powell
With: Wendy Hiller, Roger Livesey, Pamela Brown, Walter Hudd, Finlay Currie, Jean Cadell
Celtic magic undoes determined English girl.

JEANNIE (1941)
Director: Harold French
With: Barbara Mullen, Wilfred Lawson, Michael Redgrave
Scots girl and suitors.

JOHN PAUL JONES (1959)
Director: John Farrow
With: Robert Stack, Charles Coburn, Marisa Pavan, Bette Davis
Galloway-born but American hero.

KIDNAPPED (1938)
Director: Alfred Werker *With:* Warner Baxter, Freddie Batholemew, Arleen Whelan, John Carradine, Nigel Bruce
Stevenson abandoned.

KIDNAPPED (1948)
Director: William Beaudine
With: Dan O'Herlihy, Roddy McDowall, Sue England
Stevenson on the cheap.

KIDNAPPED (1959)
Director: Robert Stevenson *With:* Peter Finch, James MacArthur, Bernard Lee, John Laurie, Finlay Currie, Peter O'Toole
Disney takes to the heather with Breck and Balfour.

KIDNAPPED (1971)
Director: Delbert Mann *With:* Michael Caine, Trevor Howard, Jack Hawkins, Gordon Jackson, Vivien Heilbron
Once more into the heather.

THE KIDNAPPERS (1953)
Director: Philip Leacock
With: Duncan Macrae, Jean Anderson, Adrienne Corri, Theodore Bikel, Jon Whiteley, Vincent Winter
Cute Scottish kids in Nova Scotia.

LAXDALE HALL (1952)
Director: John Eldridge
With: Ronald Squire, Kathleen Ryan, Raymond Huntley, Sebastian Shaw, Fulton Mackay, Roddy Macmillan
Comic antics in the Highlands.

LET'S BE HAPPY (1957)
Director: Henry Levin
With: Vera-Ellen, Tony Martin, Zena Marshall, Robert Flemyng
Jeannie again, Vera-Ellen returns to Edinburgh.

THE LIFE OF ROBERT BURNS (1926)
Director: Maurice Sandground
With: Wal Croft, Craigie Brown
Our national bard.

THE LIFE OF SIR WALTER SCOTT (1926)
Director: Maurice Sandground
Our national novelist.

LIFE OF STUFF (1997)
Director: Simon Donald
With: Mabel Aitken, Ewen Bremner, Liam Cunningham, Jason Flemyng, Ciaran Hinds, Gina McKee
Stage hit flops on screen.

THE LITTLE MINISTER (1921)
Director: Penrhyn Stanlaws *With:* Betty Compson, George Hackathorne
Silent Barrie.

THE LITTLE MINISTER (1934)
Director: Richard Wallace
With: Katharine Hepburn, John Beal, Alan Hale, Donald Crisp, Lumsden Hare, Andy Clyde, Beryl Mercer
Ancient Barrie whimsy.

LIVING APART TOGETHER (1983)
Director: Charles Gormley
With: B A Robertson, Barbara
Kellerman, Jimmy Logan, Peter Capaldi
Rock singer back home.

LOCAL HERO (1983)
Director: Bill Forsyth
With: Burt Lancaster, Peter Riegert,
Denis Lawson, Peter Capaldi,
Fulton Mackay, Jenny Seagrove
Big businessman encounters big beach,
big sky.

LOCH NESS (1996)
Director: John Henderson
With: Ted Danson, Joely Richardson,
Ian Holm, Harris Yulin, Kirsty Graham
American scientist seeks explanation,
falls for Scotland.

**THE LOVES OF MARY QUEEN
OF SCOTS (1923)**
Director: Denison Clift
With: Fay Compton, Gerald Ames
Noble lady suffers.

**THE LOVES OF ROBERT BURNS
(1930)**
Director: Herbert Wilcox
With: Joseph Hislop, Dorothy
Seacombe
Rabbie sings.

LUCIA (1998)
Director: Don Boyd *With:* Amanda
Boyd, Richard Coxon, Mark Holland,
Ann Taylor, Jimmy Logan
Scott, Donnizetti, in modern setting.

MACBETH (1948)
Director: Orson Welles
With: Orson Welles, Jeanette Nolan,
Dan O' Herlihy, Roddy McDowall,
Edgar Barrier, Alan Napier
Bard burrs on cardboard hillside.

MACBETH (1972)
Director: Roman Polanski
With: Jon Finch, Francesca Annis,
Martin Shaw, Paul Shelley
Young up-and-coming couple come
unstuck.

MADELEINE (1949)
Director: David Lean
With: Ann Todd, Ivan Desny, Norman
Wooland, Leslie Banks, Elizabeth Sellars
Did Miss Smith do it?

THE MAGGIE (1954)
Director: Alexander MacKendrick
With: Paul Douglas, Alex Mackenzie,
James Copeland, Abe Barker,
Tommy Kearins
Exasperated American loosens up
on puffer.

**MAIRI, THE ROMANCE OF A
HIGHLAND MAIDEN (1912)**
Director: Andrew Paterson
With: Evelyn Duguid, Dan Munro,
Jack Maguire
Love triangle on the coast.

A MAN CALLED PETER (1955)
Director: Henry Koster
With: Richard Todd, Jean Peters,
Marjorie Rambeau, Jill Esmond,
Les Tremayne
Manse to White House.

MARIGOLD (1938)
Director: Thomas Bentley
With: Sophie Stewart, Patrick Barr,
Nicholas Hannen, Phyllis Dare,
Jean Clyde
Bonnet drama in Victorian Edinburgh.

MARY OF SCOTLAND (1936)
Director: John Ford
With: Katharine Hepburn,
Fredric March, Florence Eldridge,
Douglas Walton, John Carradine
Lassie came home.

**MARY QUEEN OF SCOTS
(1972)**
Director: Charles Jarrott
With: Vanessa Redgrave, Glenda
Jackson, Patrick McGoohan, Timothy
Dalton, Nigel Davenport, Trevor
Howard
Tall blonde has no luck with men
or cousin.

**THE MASTER OF BALLANTRAE
(1953)**
Director: William Keighley
With: Errol Flynn, Roger Livesey,
Anthony Steel, Beatrice Campbell,
Felix Aylmer, Mervyn Johns,
Yvonne Furneaux
Unlikely brothers fall out over war
and women.

MRS BROWN (1997)
Director: John Madden
With: Judi Dench, Billy Connolly,
Anthony Sher, Geoffrey Palmer
Victoria likes a bit of rough.

MY CHILDHOOD (1972)
MY AIN FOLK (1973)
MY WAY HOME (1978)
Director: Bill Douglas *With:* Stephen Archibald, Hugh Restorick, Jean Taylor-Smith, Karl Fieseler, Bernard McKenna, Paul Kermack, Helena Gloag, Ann Smith, Eileen McCallum,
Unhappy childhood, hope and love as adult.

MY LIFE SO FAR (1999)
Director: Hugh Hudson *With:* Colin Firth, Mary Elizabeth Mastrantonio, Malcolm McDowell, Rosemary Harris, Irene Jacob, Kelly MacDonald
Eccentric Scots gentry.

MY NAME IS JOE (1998)
Director: Ken Loach *With:* Peter Mullan, Louise Goodall, David McKay, Anne-Marie Kennedy, David Hayman
Former alcoholic meets social worker, love blossoms.

THE NEAR ROOM (1995)
Director: David Hayman *With:* Adrian Dunbar, David O'Hara, David Hayman, Tom Watson, Julie Graham
Glasgow underworld.

ONE MORE KISS (1999)
Director: Vadim Jean
With: Valerie Edmond, Gerard Butler, James Cosmo, Valerie Gogan
Terminal illness, final romance on Tweed.

ORPHANS (1997)
Director: Peter Mullan
With: Douglas Henshall, Gary Lewis, Stephen McCole, Frank Gallagher, Alex Norton
Stormy family funeral.

OWD BOB (1938)
Director: Robert Stevenson
With: Will Fyffe, Margaret Lockwood, John Loder
Star turn as old shepherd.

PEGGY (1916)
Director: Thomas Ince
With: Billie Burke,
William H Thompson
New York girl returns home to shock.

PLAY ME SOMETHING (1989)
Director: Timothy Neat
With: John Berger, Tilda Swinton, Hamish Henderson, Margaret Bennett, Liz Lochhead
Storyteller entertains at Barra airport.

THE PRIDE OF THE CLAN (1917)
Director: Maurice Tourneur
With: Mary Pickford, Matt Moore, Warren Cooke
America's sweetheart is clan chieftain.

THE PRIME OF MISS JEAN BRODIE (1968)
Director: Ronald Neame
With: Maggie Smith, Robert Stephens, Pamela Franklin, Gordon Jackson, Celia Johnson
Sparky schoolteacher inspires gels, but horrifies Head.

QUENTIN DURWARD (1955)
Director: Richard Thorpe
With: Robert Taylor, Kay Kendall, Robert Morley, Alec Clunes,
Marius Goring, Ernest Thesiger
Scots knight woos fiery lady in Low Countries.

RATCATCHER (1999)
Director: Lynne Ramsay
With: Bill Eadie, Tommy Flanagan, Mandy Matthews, Michelle Stewart, Lynne Ramsay jnr
Govan childhood, poetic treatment.

RED ENSIGN (1934)
Director: Michael Powell
With: Leslie Banks, Carol Goodner, Frank Vosper, Alfred Drayton, John Laurie
Clydebank rivalry.

REGENERATION (1997)
Director: Gillies Mackinnon
With: James Wilby, Stuart Bunce, Jonny Lee Miller, Jonathan Pryce, John Neville, Dougray Scott
Broken minds in World War I hospital.

RESTLESS NATIVES (1985)
Director: Michael Hoffman
With: Vincent Friell, Joe Mullaney, Teri Lally, Ned Beatty, Robert Urquhart
Clever lads rob tourists.

RING OF BRIGHT WATER (1969)
Director: Jack Couffer
With: Bill Travers, Virginia McKenna, Peter Jeffrey, Roddy Macmillan, Jameson Clark, Jean Taylor-Smith, Archie Duncan
Highland couple tame local wildlife.

ROB ROY (1911)
Director: Arthur Vivian
With: John Clyde, Theo Henries, Durward Lely
Britain's first big screen hero.

ROB ROY (1995)
Director: Michael Caton-Jones
With: Liam Neeson, Jessica Lange,
John Hurt, Tim Roth, Eric Stoltz,
Brian Cox
Thrills in the hills.

**ROB ROY: THE HIGHLAND
ROGUE (1953)**
Director: Harold French
With: Richard Todd, Glynis Johns,
James Robertson-Justice, Michael
Gough, Finlay Currie, Jean Taylor-
Smith, Geoffrey Keen, Archie Duncan
Knees run riot on the hillside.

ROCKETS GALORE (1958)
Director: Michael Relph
With: Finlay Currie, Jeannie Carson,
Donald Sinden, Roland Culver,
Noel Purcell
Not whisky this time, but …

RULER OF THE SEAS (1939)
Director: Frank Lloyd
With: Will Fyffe, Douglas Fairbanks jnr,
Margaret Lockwood
Clydesiders race to cross the ocean.

SEVEN DAYS LEAVE (1930)
Director: Richard Wallace, John
Cromwell
With: Gary Cooper, Beryl Mercer,
Daisy Belmore
Barrie's old lady claims Coop.

SHALLOW GRAVE (1994)
Director: Danny Boyle
With: Ewan McGregor, Kerry Fox,
Christopher Eccleston, Kevin Allen
Corpse and fortune in the New Town.

**SHEPHERD LASSIE OF ARGYLE
(1914)**
Director: Larry Trimble
With: Florence Turner, Rex Davis
Title tells it all.

THE SHIPBUILDERS (1943)
Director: John Baxter
With: Clive Brook, Morland Graham,
Finlay Currie
Clydeside propaganda.

SHIPYARD SALLY (1939)
Director: Monty Banks
With: Gracie Fields, Sydney Howard,
Morton Selten
Our Gracie as Clydeside pub landlady.

SILENT SCREAM (1989)
Director: David Hayman
With: Ian Glenn, Paul Samson, Andrew
Barr, Robert Carlyle, Anne Kirsten
Barlinnie on screen.

THE SILVER DARLINGS (1947)
Director: Clarence Elder, Clifford Evans
With: Clifford Evans, Helen Shingler,
Carl Bernard
Gunn's herring saga.

THE SLAB BOYS (1997)
Director: John Byrne
With: Russell Barr, Louise Berry, Bill
Gardiner, Moray Hunter, Robin Laing,
David O'Hara
1957 Paisley lads in a carpet factory.

SMALL FACES (1996)
Director: Gillies Mackinnon *With:* Ian
Robertson, Joseph McFadden, Clare
Higgins, J S Duffy, Kevin McKidd
Tough life for boys in 1960s Glasgow.

**SOFT TOP HARD SHOULDER
(1992)**
Director: Stefan Schwartz *With:* Peter
Capaldi, Elaine Collins, Phyllis Logan,
Simon Callow, Richard Wilson
Road movie for writer/star/driver.

THE SPY IN BLACK (1939)
Director: Michael Powell *With:* Conrad
Veidt, Valerie Hobson, Sebastian Shaw,
Marius Goring, June Duprez
Who goes there in the Orkneys?

STORM IN A TEACUP (1937)
Director: Victor Saville, Ian Dalrymple
With: Vivien Leigh, Rex Harrison, Sara
Allgood, Cecil Parker, Gus McNaughton
Dog trouble for Professor Higgins and
Scarlett.

THE SWORDSMAN (1948)
Director: Joseph H Lewis
With: Larry Parks, Ellen Drew,
George MacReady, Edgar Buchanan,
Ray Collins, Marc Platt
Strife among the clans.

TAM LIN (1971)
Director: Roddy McDowall *With:* Ava
Gardner, Ian McShane, Stephanie
Beacham, Richard Wattis, Cyril Cusack,
Fabia Drake, Joanna Lumley
Lad snatched by bad woman, saved by
daughter of manse.

THAT SINKING FEELING (1979)
Director: Bill Forsyth
With: Tom Mannion, Eddie Burt,
Richard Demarco, Alex Mackenzie,
Margaret Adams, Kim Masterson,
Danny Benson, Robert Buchanan
Stainless steel sink drama.

THE THIRTY-NINE STEPS (1935)
Director: Alfred Hitchcock
With: Robert Donat, Madeleine Carroll,
Lucie Mannheim, Godfrey Tearie,
John Laurie, Peggy Ashcroft
Buchan shocker, Hitchcock genius.

THE THIRTY-NINE STEPS (1959)
Director: Ralph Thomas
With: Kenneth More, Taina Elg, Barry
Jones, James Hayter, Michael Goodliffe,
Duncan Lamont, Brenda de Banzie
Hannay runs again.

THE THIRTY-NINE STEPS (1978)
Director: Don Sharp
With: Robert Powell, David Warner,
Eric Porter, John Mills, Karen Dotrice
And again.

THIS YEAR'S LOVE (1999)
Director: David Kane
With: Douglas Henshall, Catherine
McCormack, Kathy Burke, Dougray
Scott, Jennifer Ehle, Ian Hart
On-and-off romances for exiled Scots.

THE THREE LIVES OF
THOMASINA (1963)
Director: Don Chaffey *With:* Susan
Hampshire, Patrick McGoohan, Karen
Dotrice, Vincent Winter, Laurence
Naismith, Finlay Currie
Scots cat tells tale.

TICKETS FOR THE ZOO (1991)
Director: Brian Crumlish
With: Alice Broe, Fiona Chalmers,
Mickey McPherson
Edinburgh homeless.

TRAINSPOTTING (1996)
Director: Danny Boyle
With: Ewan McGregor, Ewen Bremner,
Jonny Lee Miller, Kevin McKidd,
Robert Carlyle, Kelly MacDonald
Thin, pale young men, drugs, and jokes.

TROUBLE IN THE GLEN (1954)
Director: Herbert Wilcox *With:* Margaret
Lockwood, Orson Welles, Forrest Tucker,
Victor McLaglen, John McCallum,
Moultrie Kelsall, Margaret McCourt
Mismatching of talents in dreich
Highlands.

TUNES OF GLORY (1960)
Director: Ronald Neame *With:* Alec
Guinness, John Mills, Dennis Price,
Gordon Jackson, John Fraser, Kay Walsh,
Susannah York, Duncan Macrae
Old boys fall out in barracks.

VENUS PETER (1989)
Director: Ian Sellar
With: Ray McAnally, David Hayman,
Sinead Cusack, Gordon Strachan,
Caroline Paterson, Juliet Cadzow,
Sheila Keith
Stromness is the star.

WEDDING GROUP (1933)
Director: Alex Bryce
With: Alastair Sim, Fay Compton,
Barbara Greene, Patric Knowles,
Michael Wilding
From manse to Crimea.

WEE WILLIE WINKIE (1937)
Director: John Ford
With: Shirley Temple, Victor McLaglen,
Cesar Romero, C Aubrey Smith
Northwest Frontier saved by moppet.

WHAT EVERY WOMAN KNOWS
(1921)
Director: William De Mille
With: Lois Wilson, Conrad Nagel
Scots on the make.

WHAT EVERY WOMAN KNOWS
(1934)
Director: Gregory La Cava
With: Helen Hayes, Brian Aherne,
Donald Crisp, Madge Evans, Dudley
Digges, David Torrence
Scots on the make talk about it.

WHISKY GALORE! (1948)
Director: Alexander MacKendrick
With: Basil Radford, Joan Greenwood,
James Robertson-Justice, Gordon
Jackson, Duncan Macrae, Compton
Mackenzie, Jean Cadell, A E Matthews
Scotch on the rocks.

THE WICKER MAN (1973)
Director: Robin Hardy
With: Edward Woodward, Britt Ekland,
Diane Cilento, Ingrid Pitt, Christopher
Lee, Lesley Mackie, Walter Carr, Irene
Sunters, Lindsay Kemp
The locals are not so friendly.

THE WINTER GUEST (1997)
Director: Alan Rickman *With:* Emma
Thompson, Phyllida Law, Gary Holly-
wood, Arlene Cockburn, Sheila Reid
Mother-daughter relations in chilly Fife.

YOU'RE ONLY YOUNG TWICE
(1952)
Director: Terence Egan Bishop
With: Duncan Macrae, Charles Hawtrey,
Patrick Barr, Joseph Tomelty,
Robert Urquhart, Ronnie Corbett
Varsity romps.